# My Life Is
# FAITH
## Victory In Darkness

MARYANN NATHANIEL

MY LIFE IS FAITH

Published By Maryann Nathaniel

Copyright 2022 Maryann Nathaniel. All rights reserved.

Printed By: BookBaby

www.Bookbaby.com

Contact Author Maryann Nathaniel

@

Yieldedvessel@yahoo.com

ISBN: 978-1-66783-737-6

eBook ISBN: 978-1-66783-738-3

# CONTENTS

# INTRODUCTION

The scenery was breathtaking; the waves were coming strongly; the wind had picked up in September 2019 while I was standing at the water's edge in Wildwood Crest, New Jersey. Some sisters and I from the ministry had just come from morning worship; as I stood and gazed out, I watched as the Sun began to move behind the clouds. I began to pray, and while praying, I heard, "My life is faith." I did not understand all of what I heard at the moment. In July 2021, the Holy Spirit began to speak to me about what I heard, "My Life Is Faith" which I initially thought of was a statement He spoke to me about me. My Life Is Faith is a collection of a lifetime of moments, some of which could have ended my very life. Here, I am telling about my times of trials, tribulations, sickness, distress, victories, and triumphs to bring hope, healing, encouragement, and empowerment to help everyone who reads it. I began to retrospect my life, which allowed me to revisit some dark, painful moments of my life, which I had never shared with anyone before. Some of these times left me in an almost bitter and unforgiving state. Later in my life, I discovered that forgiveness was mandatory if I wanted to be pleasing to the Lord. Forgiveness was to free me from the pain many individuals had brought upon me. Bitterness was keeping me angry, instigating me to retaliate. The Holy Spirit began to minister to me and remind me of the things that I had faced and overcame in life. He then instructed me during July 2021 to share about my life with the world, and in doing so, many will be inspired and motivated. Something in them will break as they read and turn the pages. You will read something that is going to help you and to bring light to wherever you are in your life. It's written for you if you are struggling with your identity and the pain of your past, or if you are in doubt about your future. The Holy Spirit would then say, "It is not just a book, it is a propeller. It will thrust an individual in their life." Faith in Hebrew is EMUNAH that is defined as faith or belief that means a life full of reliance upon Jesus Christ. Allow Him to come into your life and take full control. Faith comes by hearing the Word of God. You must have total trust. Faith is the power that connects us with the spiritual realm that joins us with God. Faith is a supernatural gift from God; it is the beginning of eternal life. Through faith we can claim victory over victory, even in darkness. We cannot see faith; it dwells in our heart. We cannot have doubt if we have faith; we must believe God although we can't see Him. It affects our decisions. I have learned that listening to the promises of God would increase my faith. Having the faith to believe in any situation just as when God spoke and created the universe it was so. Every born-again believer has been given a measure of faith. Scripture tells us in John 20:29 Jesus had told John, "Because you have seen me, you have believed; blessed are those who have not seen and yet have believed." Once you decide that you will walk by faith, you must release any fear, look to the Lord, and embrace the path that He leads you down. The more I developed my relationship with God and got closer to Him, the easier it became for me to trust Him. In life we all face some challenging times; therefore, it is especially important for you to take time every day to have a conversation with our Lord and Savior Jesus Christ. When you think about FAITH, it could be defiantly challenging without having a relationship with the Master of It. It means that you will be having complete trust or confidence in someone or something you cannot see. It is often said that we do not doubt when we take a seat in a chair; we have faith or belief that it is going to hold us. We trust in God or in the doctrines of religion based on our spiritual apprehension rather than proof. Faith gives us the confidence in what we hope for and the assurance that the Lord is working, although it is not before our very eyes. Faith knows that no matter what the situation in our lives or someone else's, the Lord is working on it. When I speak My Life is FAITH, I utterly understand I only survived the dark, trying, sick days and yes, the very days when I even contemplated driving my car into buses trucks and stone walls. None of these things destroyed me, I know with my whole heart it was because of my faith. My life depends on my faith. All my life's testimonies trials and hard test I know it was because of my faith I made it through. Having walked through my life from the age of two to present and knowing that my very existence has been based on me applying biblical scriptures to my life daily throughout my journey. I have experienced the Lord through faith as the precious gift from the Holy Spirit. Truly applying what the scripture tells while mentioning that we walk by faith and not by sight!!!! Believing deep in my heart that if I were sick, I would be healed; if I were in debt, I would be financially free; if I were lost, I would be found; if I were pressured in my mind, I could cast all my cares upon the Lord; and if I was broken, I will be restored. It means always being reminded that whatever my heart desires, I will receive, and that it will be given to me through the Word of God, knowing my life is faith. In this propeller, you will see scriptures come alive through my walk, and you will see me overcome and be victorious. My life is faith is shared to propel you from the very place where you may be right now. My testimonies are shared to lead you to believe that no matter what you face in life the Lord will see you through, see Jesus Christ, and learn how to rely on the Holy Spirit. My testimonies are shared to help you believe in God at another level during the hardest times of your life, usher you into the presence of the Holy Spirit, empower you, and help you walk by faith, and not by sight. They are to lead you into prayer. They are to allow you to know that everything should be taken to the Lord in prayer and that nothing is too hard for Him.

# CHAPTER 1
## Saved From The Fire

The thought of the house turning into an inferno in the matter of minutes; the sight of the flames coming from the windows and doors; the thick, black smoke; the cries and the screams from the neighbors; and the looks of my aunt and all the children terrified in the window of the front bedroom, crying a desperate cry of reality, which later became my imagination. I often think about this incident that occurred in my life; however, because I was between the age of two and three years old, I don't have my actual memory of it. I can only imagine the scene, what it looked like and the sounds that filled the air. It was shared with me by my mother; my father never really talked about it. I'm sure, this was because it was his sister and I'm his daughter, and his emotions had left him in a confused and hurtful, yet grateful place because I was saved from the fire. For me, it's never easy to talk about it, because it always brings so many questions to my mind. At one point in my life, I use to ask myself, *was why was I saved?* The devil takes advantage of the opportunity to cause a battle in your mind—sowing the seeds of having you questioning your worth and your existence. Sometimes, in our lives, we can hold things against ourselves, things that could harm us. Choices and decisions that we made or things that might have been done to us which we had no control over that lingers on in our lives and continues to cause us more hurt and pain. The question of why was

I saved from the fire or why did that have to happen to those children and my aunt? Why did they perish in the fire? What if the phone call with my mother went another way? Wow! Just a difference of a few words could have made a difference. These questions often come to my mind, and I find myself trying to get answers to them. When you began to question difficult times in your life that left you with so much hurt the devil uses this time to cause a battle in your mind. At a young age, I felt bad; I didn't fully understand that it was nothing I could have done about the fire and that I shouldn't have felt bad about me being saved from it. I was too young to realize that I was just a toddler. What could have I done? You often start winning a battle when you realize it was out of your control. I never shared with anyone how it bothered me as a young girl, because I always thought it would bring up the bad memory of the fire with my father and I never wanted to see him hurting.

The devil tried to have his way in my mind about it. I never mentioned how I felt and what I was feeling as a little girl except with my fourth-grade teacher, who I thought was very mean. However, the truth is that she truly was beautiful inside out. I never smiled during fourth grade. I guess school was the only place where I felt I could show signs of how I was feeling. I used to suppress my feelings at home, trying not to talk about this horrible time in my family's life. After talking to Mrs. K, I remember her telling me to smile. I 'can't recall the full conversation in detail though. However, what I will always remember is what came out of our conversation. She told me to smile, and that day I did. In fact, from that day forth, all I did was smile. I believe she might have assured me that I could not do anything about it, and I shouldn't feel bad about it. She went on to tell me that I had a beautiful smile and entered me into the smiling contest that was being held that year. I went on to being the first runner up in the contest.

You can't allow things that are not within your control to ever weigh on your heart and mind, 'because that's the very thing that the devil will use. The mind is where he does the most of his fighting. These fights lead to things being held in your heart, which are not good for you. Although I can't remember my aunt Claresa because of my age at the time, I was told that she loved children and would often babysit. She had decided to start her babysitting service for people in and around her West Philly neighborhood as well as some parts of North Philly.

One weekend, she called my mother and father to ask if I could spend some time with her. She came to pick me up and took me back to my 'grandfather's house in West Philly, where they lived. I imagine that my parents, being young adults in love and desiring time alone, didn't hesitate. They allowed me to go with her. I used to wonder if the fire was the reason that later in their life, my parents were very strict about us spending the night out at a family or friend's home. I spent one night with her. My memory doesn't allow me to remember what happened during my visit. Because of her love for children and the fact that I was her niece, I'm sure we had a great time. I believe she loved and would have protected me. I also believe that she tried everything she could to protect those other children in the house during the time of the fire. It was well-known how she adored and cared for children.

The next evening, my aunt Claresa desired to take me with her on her babysitting job. My mother later shared with me she was standing in the kitchen, cleaning dishes, when the phone rang. It was Aunt Claresa on the other end of the phone, asking with excitement if I could stay with her for one more night. My mother told me that she felt something said to her, "Bring your baby home." I believe it was the Holy Spirit. She told me that while she continued cleaning the dishes, she heard again, "Bring your baby home." She didn't think twice after that. She said, "No Claresa, bring her home." My aunt said, "Mary, please can I just keep her one more night?" My mother said that a thought instantly came to her mind, and she said, "Claresa, she has a' doctor's appointment, and I want to shampoo her hair." With disappointment my aunt replied, "OK" and ended the phone call.

Aunt Claresa brought me home. Then she left to go to the house where she had to babysit that evening. My mother told me that the two of them had a brief conversation while my aunt waited for the bus. A few hours later, the telephone rang. It was my grandfather, who was currently in Virginia with his

Church for a convention. My mom told me that the first thing he asked her was, "Mary, where's my granddaughter?" She said,' "She's right here, Mr. Williams. What's wrong?" He told her that my aunt and the children for whom she was caring just perished in the fire on Page Street.

There was a time in my life when I often thought about my aunt and those children whose lives ended in that fire. The fire started from downstairs in the living room, and quickly spread throughout the house. The second floor, where they were, collapsed, and they had no chance of survival. I was told that the neighbors were yelling and screaming, telling them to jump!!! This still leaves me puzzled.... Was it that they couldn't hear them? Or did the fear of the fire paralyze them? The thought of them battling the blazes of that fire makes my stomach cringe. To know that the floor caved in, and they all went down into the fire leaves me shaking when I think of it, you would think it's nothing far more horrific as this. Did the fear of the fire paralyze them causing them to stand still? From the many things I got out of tragedy is this one thing that stands out and has helped me throughout life. Never allow a harsh experience to bring fear that can cause you to doubt your way of escape!!!

I can't help but think that because my parents were young adults, they would have enjoyed the time alone. The one more night when my aunt Claresa pleaded to take me with her could have been the very last night my parents would have had me. I'm forever thankful and grateful to the Lord because my mother followed through with what she was feeling at the time.... What if she would have let me stay one more night? As I grew older and began to look at life, I have always had a deep appreciation for the life that has been given to me. At any moment, a split-second decision could have been the end of my life. Living with knowing the fact that I was just a phone call away from not being here today, this became my testimony at a time I didn't even know what a testimony was! Having a testimony at the age of three makes me think about life with appreciation every day!!

Scripture reminds me that life is like a vapor. It appears for a little time, and then it vanishes away. Vapor ... Wow, it's like a mist. After hearing in your life at any moment, you could have been gone from this world in such a tragic way it helps you understand when the scripture tells us life can vanish so quickly. My mother tells me that my aunt was burned beyond recognition; she was identified through dental records. Because she was burned so badly, a beautiful picture of her was placed on her closed coffin. I remember my grandfather showing me that picture when I was a teenager. Her beautiful smile illuminated in that picture. I used to pause and think, saying, "It must be someone greater." Instantly acknowledging the Lord for my life and being saved from the fire. Then the devil brings the thoughts and questions in my mind, such as *Why wasn't anyone else saved from the fire?* Suddenly a peace would come over me, and I would find myself saying, *it was a tragic accident.* Then I think about the devil and how he comes to steal, kill, and destroy!! When I reached the age in life to know I knew I had to give my life back to the one who saved me from the fire. This was one of the things that always made me know that there is a God, and not just any god.

Whatever you do, give the Lord glory for your LIFE!! Although I was taken to Church as child, it wasn't until my encounter with the Holy Spirit that I was able to identify who He was. As my personal relationship developed with the Lord, I knew that the incident when He saved me from the fire must have been the very thing that had drawn me closer to him. I began to see that it was He who had guided my mother in that conversation. It took me some years to realize what had happened. Although I never had the opportunity to know my aunt, it's a blessing to know that she knew me and was able to hold me. The most beautiful part about this is that I know she as well as all those other children who had perished in the fire are being held by our Father in Heaven. The frequent thought of what would have happened if my mother wouldn't have listened to the voice brings always bring me to tears. I understand that in life there would always be some questions you will never get answers to, however all you can do is seek the Holy Spirit for comfort and TRUST THE LORD.

Over forty years later, I see the name in writing who kept me from the fire. I sometimes go to the hair salon near the place that had caught fire. One spring morning, I decided to go to the hair salon. I arrived early, and as I parked, the

Holy Spirit whispered, "Look up…." When I did, what I saw instantly took me to a place of praise and worship!!!! I was parked directly in front of Page Street, the block where I was saved from the fire. I looked down and saw my Lord and Savior's name—Jesus!!!! Yes, Jesus!!! Five flowerpots, each bearing one letter painted of His name JESUS lined up on the block where the fire was. I can't describe all that happened to me while sitting in my car. My imagination kicked in, trying to visualize the fire. I began to sing that it could have been me!!! Immediately, I thought of my aunt and those other children!!! Right now, I'm giving the Lord glory Hallelujah. He saved me from the fire—physically, as a toddler, and spiritually, as a young adult.

As a young adult I learned "The Lord will allow things to happen in your life that you will never fully understand; however, He places your purpose in life down on the inside of you." Yes, I understand that there had to be a plan and purpose for my life, never ever thinking that there wasn't a plan for my aunt and those other children. Learning that there was a purpose for my life early helped me mentally as I often thought about it. Only the Lord Himself was able to do that. Only He could have touched my heart and mind.

As I reflect on this, I think about the time when Pharaoh ordered all the first-born male babies to be killed. Moses's mother placed him in a basket and gently pushed him away in the Nile River, because she knew he was in harm's way. Only the wisdom of God along with the love she had for her son could have made her do that. A mother's love will protect her baby. Her obedience resulted in Moses being saved. Our obedience can be life-changing and for sure lifesaving! It shows our faith and trust in God. It's the key that unlocks our blessings and leads us to success. The more I asked the Holy Spirit to fill me up with His love and Spirit, the more obedient I have become. The Bible tells us to TRUST in the Lord with all our hearts and lean not to our own understanding. In all your ways, acknowledge the Lord, and He shall direct your path.

I'm thankful that my mother knew the Lord enough that He had empowered her with His Spirit. As a young woman, my mother believed it was something she just came up with, because she admits that I never actually had a doctor's appointment. Later in life, her choice of words changed as she began to say, "I know God is real." I truly believe that the Holy Spirit gave the thought to her about me having a doctor's appointment!! All glory and honor go to Him.... He knows our beginning, middle, and ending. It's very important that you allow the Holy Spirit to lead you. You must get in a place of prayer, seek the Holy Spirit, and remain there until He pours out upon you. It is because my mother had listened to the voice that came from deep within her and her obedience that I got saved from the fire. I will encourage you to obey the voice of the Holy Spirit. He guides and directs us.

# CHAPTER 2

## My Identity Identified

A few years later my mother and father had a beautiful baby girl and named her after my aunt Claresa. As the years went on, my grandfather, Deida, always made sure that I had an ample supply of paper and pencils. My sister Claresa and I spent almost every weekend with him. He never stopped me from using my imagination. I believe in my heart that he knew the purpose of it all. If he was here today, I'm sure he would have confirmed that it wasn't my imagination and that I was dreaming and having visions. As I got older, around ten or eleven years of age, my grandfather and I used to sit down and talk. He would share with me how I used to play with tops for hours. Sounds strange right? He would often remind me how, around the age of four, I always wanted my play area to be set up as if it was a classroom. The interesting part about that was that I hadn't even started going to school yet. Where did I get the thought from?

This was something that, I'm sure, many other children may have been doing as well, however, I always believed, after fully understanding what was going on, that it was a connecting piece in my life. I understood the things I was doing had meaning and purpose. Thinking about how I would just sit and talk, I wondered what I was talking about and whom I was talking to! While pretending to be a teacher I was being prepared to stand and speak to people. When I think about it, I am reminded about how God already put down in us everything before He placed us in our mother's womb. He already knew who we were and who we are destined to be. His Divine Purpose for our lives was etched in the seed. When I reflect on my life as a child, I tell the Lord, "Thank you, for preparing me as a little girl!!"

My next-door neighbor, Mrs. Seymour, use to sit on her porch and talk to me about her position as a teacher. She was always excited about the school year ending!! I'll never forget her expressions as well as her relief around that time of the year!! At the end of every school year, she would give me books to read and notepads to write in. One of the things I hold dear to my heart is a book that she had given to me prior to her passing away. I didn't realize what type of book it was; it wasn't just any book she had given me. I noticed that it was a Bible concordance. She had said to me, "One day you're going to be a teacher." I didn't pay much attention to it at the time she said it. She paused, looked at me, and said, "I don't know what kind of teacher you'll be or where, all I know and believe is that you're going to be a good one."

One summer evening, I was sitting out on the porch, thinking about how she used to come out, recline in her chair, and talk the night away. I remember saying to myself, *A teacher? Am I going to be a teacher? What kind of teacher?* Going back to the beginning, when I was always sitting in that corner with objects, bottle tops, paper, pencils, crayons, and whatever it was, I would just sit in the circle and talk for hours. My parents never stopped me. How precious is the Holy Spirit when He wouldn't allow my parents to put a stop to something that most people found to be strange.

When I reflect on this part of my life, I'm able to see that it was the beginning of my preparation. I began to believe I was a teacher, or I should say that I began to embrace the teacher in me. Never allow anyone or anything to stop you from dreaming!!! My siblings had now started to join me in our middle room!! Now I had human beings instead of tops, pencils, crayons, and pens!!! Oh! How excited I was!! It's amazing when you tap into your identity. I was able to see and understand the teacher, although I didn't know what kind of teacher it was the fact that I finally began to embrace the teacher in me!! Instead of talking to imaginary people, I was now talking to real people. From the age of four to five to the tender age of ten, eleven, and twelve, "playing school" is what I called it. Being a teacher daily is what I desired. I remember coming home from school, pretending to be one of my teachers!! Every time I went to one of my family members' houses, I would always get all the children to pretend with me that we were playing school. I would find myself getting upset if they didn't want to join me. When you begin to identify your identity, you don't allow anything to hinder you.

As I continued to grow up things began to become clearer. I still didn't understand what was really happening in my life. I would have my cousins and friends' attention for hours, just as I did as a little girl, while playing with the bottle tops. During this time, while transiting into my teenage years, I was called strange. Some even said that I was different. At one point, I was even called special. I pause here to tell you that when you're called different, REJOICE in it, because you are!! The Word of God tells us that we are supposed to be different. I'm so thankful today that I never took offense to people calling me strange. If I was going to become a teacher from being called strange, I would use it as a steppingstone to push me for achieving my dream. Finally, I began to see what my life was becoming. It's simply amazing to note when your life begins to change—you begin to go through the transition and see the transformation. It's mind-blowing as I began *Identifying my Identity*

Being called strange was like seeds being planted in my mind and heart that would eventually be watered by life and push me to make my identity a reality. Be mindful of how you allow people to speak over you, and, most importantly, how you apply it to your life. Don't allow it to kill the real you that's down on the inside. Our Creator designed you for His glory and His purpose. Being called strange was a part of the process of embracing my identity. There are some things in your life that you will have to accept, because they are truly a part of you!!!

It can be very challenging for some, because it's often looked at as if you're being picked on. Remember to pause, pray, and ask the Holy Spirit to show you the real YOU!!! Don't miss the fact that He shows us who we are and who we are destined to be early in life, however we sometimes miss it because of the pressure that leads us to having an identity crisis. Seek the Holy Spirit who speaks to us and ask Him to reveal your identity!

Later in my life, I had to walk sometimes with my eyes closed. What I was seeing was overwhelming, the hurt and the pain that people were dealing with in their lives. I didn't understand the gift that was attached to the teacher. Although I embraced the teacher in me, I had to also accept the fact that my eyes were special. I was too young to understand I was as a seer. It was difficult for me in the early stages of my gift being developed. I would have dreams and nightmares about snakes and spiders, all at the same time. One dream that I can still see so very clearly is that of this long snake in my bed. I realized then that I had to always be aware of the devil who is always trying to get next to me. His desire was to try to put fear in me. He knew that if I allowed fear to settle in, then it would hinder my progress or prevent me from being who I was created to be. He tried to destroy my identity with the attempt of trying to use all the distractions that came into my life. That's what his role was in my life. I would dream about something, and it would happen. I always paid attention to my dreams, because the Holy Spirit would cause a shaken deep down on the inside of me. I understood that He was either showing me or making me aware of something.

I was hesitant to share the gift of being able to see into the lives of people, because they already thought that I was strange as a little girl. It wasn't until I had a dream of a man who called my name, took me up on this high platform, and told me to look down. When I looked down, I saw a multitude of people. He told me to tell him what I was seeing, and then he placed what appeared to be a scroll in my mouth. I will never forget that dream. It was scary yet breathtaking. I woke up knowing that there was more to my life because the scroll appeared to have messages on it that I would one day share with people. This led me to seek the Lord even in the state I was in—confused, unable to understand what all was happening. I was having an identity crisis at a very young age.

As I got older, it seemed as if it was hard for people to understand me. I couldn't help but ask myself, *Is it me?* I'm thankful to the Lord that He didn't allow the devil to mentally disturb me with this. There are times when people can't identify with who you are. They will try to have you think twice or even three times about yourself. What it did for me was that it forced me to start looking deeper into Maryann. And, of course, I began to seek out what I was being labeled as … strange, weird, unusual, odd, and PECULIAR!! Was I behaving in an unusual way? Did I come from a different place or from a different world? It can be difficult when you have a battle going on in your mind, all while trying to deny who you really are. I knew who I was however I tried to deny it because I didn't want to face what people would think of me.

The Word of God tells us that we are a chosen generation, a royal priesthood, a holy nation, and PECULIAR people. That should show forth the praises of Him who has called us out of darkness into His marvelous light. When people begin to call you names and make these statements about you, it will leave you offended, and you would not know how to respond to what is being said to you. I was told as a little girl I was always to be found somewhere in a corner playing and talking with bottle caps or something small, acting as if they were people. Because of this I was called strange, many people didn't know what was happening with me, however, my mother and father never stopped me. I guess they believed that I was keeping myself occupied.

You may have heard many voices in your life—some good, some bad, and some even traumatizing. You may have been told that you were never going to amount to anything, you were going to be useless, or you didn't have what it takes. Some may have called you bad evil names. This may have left you in the place where you are today—a place of not knowing who you are and what your purpose is. Allow these to be seeds, allow life to water them, and seek the Lord for your identity. If you feel stuck, hindered, oppressed, or depressed, take a deep breath right now and look up and say, "Speak Lord!!!!" Ask Him to take you to the place in Him where your Identity will be identified.

We are created in the image of God the Father, Son, and Holy Spirit. When you came into this world, your identity was already identified. The Trinity knows who and what they created you to be in life. We get hit with things in this world that cause us to be confused about who we are and who we are created to be. Neither did the Trinity change its mind nor did they make a mistake. It is Heaven where we must bombard with prayer about our existence. Child molestation; rape; mental, verbal, and physical abuse, etc. All are traumatizing things that would try to change who you are from within. They may try to alter you. Therefore, you must dig deep within and allow these things to come out of you. Break the silence, because the silence has kept the real you silent. However, it can never change who you were created to be. There is a part of you that's still waiting to be revealed.

Allow the Holy Spirit to operate in your life to bring healing and comfort. The Holy Spirit will breathe new breath in you. Experiencing life changes and difficulties can sometimes knock the very breath out of you. Rely on the one who knows you from inside out. The one who knows the number of hairs on your head, your fingerprints, your heartbeat, and your brain waves. The one who says that He knows the very intent of your heart. It's Him who knows all about you. He knows all about everything that you have been through, are going through, and will go through.

In fact, He has already equipped you for whatever you may go through in life. No one else can go through your hurt, pain, disappointments, setbacks, betrayal the way that you will, because it was only designed for you to go through it. Know the things that are used in your life to build you up and know the things that are meant to be used to tear you apart. I realized I was called strange because of who I was. I learned I was a seer—one who has spiritual eyes. Having an aha moment of now understanding why I was able to foresee the future and what was happening in the present … and being able to help people heal from their pass. These seeds were planted to identify my identity. Identity is often identified after you have gone through an experience of going through a crushing season. This season allows the very thing that is hidden down on the inside of you to be produced. During this season, you sometimes go through battles that you are not able to explain. In this season, you are lonely, misunderstood, and even stripped of some things that were holding you back, however, you did not realize they were. It was especially important for me to understand during the season of crushing when I did not feel good and needed to keep my eyes on Jesus and Jesus alone. When the enemy does not want you to discover your identity you will be faced with every type of attack that you can imagine. He will attack you in your mind, health, family, on your job, any place where he can cause a distraction. You would then find yourself, going through spiritual warfare fighting against the work of evil forces, spirits and demons, and while going through this is when your identity will be identified. You become aware of the very things that the enemy is fighting you for. The very things that he does not want exposed to the world. He knows those very things that are planted down inside of you, and as soon as they are exposed to light, they will be identified, and once they are identified, they're used as power. This power which causes production leads to producing the real you. During the production which is when the Lord is developing you is also the time when you are produced and once, you are produced the Lord puts you on display for his use. This is what the enemy does not want. When my identity was identified, I was able to get to the place of being a yielded vessel for our Lord and Savior Jesus Christ. When you come into the knowing of who you are, then you begin to operate in your identity. My discovery of who I was brought out all of who I am which delivered the best of me.

# CHAPTER 3
## Disliked Without A Cause

I always wanted to see people for who they were and to see them at their very best. Never was I concerned if a person appeared to have more than or better than me. I celebrated with everyone. I was always concerned about people when they were going through hard times. My desire was to be a help them, even if I needed help myself. I guess that's why it bothered me the way that it did, leaving me confused at one point in my life causing me to become distant and developing an issue of trusting people. I often wondered why after helping people through whatever they were going through why they would always turn against me.

I had to catch myself, because it was causing me to have little pebbles in my heart which was leading to the hardening of it. These pebbles were thoughts of getting back at people for the way they treated me. I later discovered that it was not good for me. I'm grateful I began to understand that it wasn't the way that I wore my hair or the way I walked or talked, but it was truly about who I was. It was still very difficult for me to understand until I prayed about it.

Through prayer, I received in my spirit to remain true to the real you. I couldn't allow people to cause me to become someone who I wasn't. One of the main reasons people dislike you without a cause is because they don't know who they themselves are. They have a problem identifying themselves. The issue is not you. During this time, the Lord protected me in a very special way. If I had allowed the evilness of people linger in my life, I wouldn't have been able to walk in the fullness of my identity. I remember sitting with myself and hearing, "Focus on your identity." It was then that the Lord continued to shape and mold me. While going through this season in my life, there was a lot of hurt and pain. I was constantly reminded, "Through all of this, remember the qualities that are on the inside of you." When I saw people hurt, I wanted to see them healed; when I saw them having doubtful feelings, I wanted to encourage them; when I saw them sick, I wanted to see them well; when I saw them in trouble, I wanted to see them get out of it; when I saw them in bondage, I wanted to see them embrace freedom; and when I saw them in a struggle, I would try to stay with them and to walk them through.

I was always telling people that no matter what was going on in their lives, they should just push through, pray, and believe that they will succeed. I used to tell them, "Whatever you do, DON'T GIVE UP!!!" There were some moments when I would find myself in a place where I knew I would overcome the situation, however, I felt defeated!!! When I had moments like these, I had to remind myself of what I would always say to people... Don't give up!! Being disliked without a cause left me feeling very confused sometimes. I realized when I became confused about anything in my life, it would lead me to get into a place of becoming withdrawn. That is what I called it then, not realizing that I was being pulled into a place of prayer. It was in this place where I was able to understand why some people did not like me. I was being disliked because of who I was; the seed of dislike was being planted to be watered by the behavior of people, some of which was very painful. This pain almost caused me to withdraw from people. Which I came to know is what the devil's plan was. He desired to shut me down which eventually would have hindered me from becoming who the Lord had created me to be.

As I got older, I began to see and understand who Maryann was. I began to get better when I started accepting the fact that I was uniquely different. Because I always struggled with being a seer, I often found myself fighting the fact that I was able to see things and know what was happening around me.

Because of the gift of being a seer I was found to be strange. I knew that people really didn't know their reason for disliking me. The demonic spirits did not want them to embrace who I was. Those spirits knew the anointing on my life would bring healing to them.

As I grew in my FAITH, I began to realize that it was never about me, but it was about the spirit of the Lord that was on the inside of me. If people would have just embraced it, they would not have had to fight the fights in their lives as hard. They did not want to accept the fact that they had issues within themselves; later in life, I started calling it "issues in their tissues"!! They did not want to accept the fact that they were going against their own selves. When people wake up every day with a frown on their face, then it's because they are battling something within themselves.

One thing in life we should do is look in the mirror and do a self-examination. We often see people walk away from relationships, friendships, etc. without giving a reason or at least sharing with you what they think might have been the reason, because most of the times they realize that they themselves were the issue, and not you. I began to bounce back from people walking away from our relationships, friendships, and fellowships as I identified who I was. I began to see and understand that when you are called out by the Lord, you will experience things that will sometimes leave you with many questions. When I began to identify my identity, I began to say to myself, "My life is not my own." I did not allow the dislike to destroy my destiny!

In the Bible, we see that we wrestle not against flesh and blood but principalities and wickedness in high places. I was able to move forward and begin to talk about how Jesus had to walk away from fights and how He wasn't accepted in His own country. When He was in danger or in the midst of people who disliked Him without a cause, He always had a way of escape. I can imagine that Jesus might have felt alone plenty of times, but then I think about how He was never alone because He always kept His eyes on His Father. He knew His purpose for coming into the Earth. He could have been amidst of people who were screaming and chanting to crucify him, and yet He would have been able to walk right through them.

In my life, I began to move in the crowded rooms where I was despised. Neither did I allow the actions of others to affect me any longer nor did I allow it to stop me. You can't allow the behavior of other people to stop you. You must keep moving, pushing, and praying. I had to remain focused and understand that people were only there to cause a setback in my life. But I had to keep believing. Why? Because I had learned why I was placed here, and I knew that I had a purpose and a destiny to reach.

Repeatedly reminding myself that my life was not my own, I had to walk through some things with my eyes closed, because looking at their faces would sometimes make me angry. I had to believe in who the Lord was creating me to be—walking through the valley of the shadow of death and fearing no evil, because the Lord's rod and His staff was there to comfort me. He prepared a table before me in the presence of my enemies, and He anointed my head with oil. I did not understand why I was enduring so much. However the Lord always comforted me and made my cup to run over. I know goodness and mercy follows me all the days of my life. And therefore, MY LIFE IS FAITH.

My faith tells me to follow it all the days of my life and I will dwell in the house of the Lord forever. I learned that I must remain steadfast, unmovable, and always abounding in the work of the Lord, so I kept my focus on being a teacher, and it kept me grounded. However, I didn't know what kind of teacher I would be. How could you teach anybody how to be healed if you haven't walked through a healing process yourself? How could you teach how to love if you yourself don't know how to love? So, I kept my mind focused on the thought that I was destined to be a teacher and I was going to be the best teacher I was being called to be.

I had to continue to walk by faith, and not by sight. It helped me to know that MY LIFE IS FAITH. I was able to embrace my true purpose and know my destiny!!!! I could walk in it. Had I not understood what it meant to be disliked without a cause, I would not have been able to escape the tricks, schemes, plots, and the plans of the devil. It only happens when you get to that place of acknowledging your identity. When you can get to that place of knowing, you fully understand what it means being disliked without a cause.

*Being disliked without a cause* or having to come to a place of awareness that you will be disliked without a cause in this life is a very hard place to be, especially for a young teenager. Hence, I started trying to figure things out and *DIGGING* deep down on the inside of me, all while searching the real me. Going through the time of being mistreated, lied on, you know, all the things that come along with being despised, I used to wonder why there was so much hostility toward me and why people were acting in such a way without a cause. Although it troubled me very much, but I always found a way to get past this and continued with a purpose of finding out who I was.

# CHAPTER 4

## Loved But Not Loved

**Growing up in the heart** of North Philadelphia with two loving parents, a decent block, and beautiful people, I used to watch neighbors move in and out. My parents never allowed us to hang out in the neighborhood, but only to school, store, and visit my grandfather's house nearby. My sister and I could only ride our bikes from one end of the block to the next. We would switch from our bikes to our roller skates now and then. We weren't allowed to leave the block. Between the age of fifteen and sixteen we were supposed to abide by the rules that were placed in our home and never to question them. When the streetlights were turned on, we knew it was time to go in. Seven days a week, same routine!!

I often wondered what everyone else was doing around the corner at the schoolyard or at the recreation center aka (THE REC). Oh, how I would have loved to know. I would dread the spring, summer and sometimes even the fall knowing that we couldn't participate in what was happening in our neighborhood. One time I was so frustrated with it that I started thinking of ways to escape. Now, I'm having a moment while laughing about it. I realized that my parents were doing what was best for us.

As I got older, I began to have conversations with different people getting to know them. I started to feel like I was becoming a part of what was around me. I began to experience some of the things that I saw some of the girls of my age experience, going out and mingling with neighborhood associates. Some of the young men in our neighborhood looked out for us, and they really did. They would make sure that we were okay when we went to the store or to my grandfather's house. They would wait for me to go to the store to get my attention. However, my father was always a protector of us. He didn't allow me to have conversations with boys and men.

Then I reached the age when I was able to start leaving off the block. The attention and distractions remained. I started responding to my name being called. I began to engage in conversations with boys & men, they started asking for my phone number or if they could come sit with me. I remember everything happening so fast when I had begun yielding to the attention.

*LOVED BUT NOT LOVED!* Many loved what they saw—the beautiful girl with a pretty smile, who was sitting on the front steps of her parent's home. They loved what they saw, and they were drawn to it. I was paying attention to the attention that was being given to me. Responding to the attention, I began to allow people to occupy my space. I allowed myself to get to a place where I didn't understand the love, which I came to know wasn't love. I began to accept the lies and the manipulation thinking that it was a part of love. "Loved but not loved" … wow I used to think about it in many different areas of my life regarding friendships and relationships.

I've dealt with that part of my heart that could have destroyed me. I thought I was being loved, but the love wasn't love, it was just lust. The experience of what seemed to be ten years was only two years.

From the tender age of sixteen to eighteen, I allowed people to act like they loved me. I was able to see very early when the devil was trying to strip my identity. Yes, strip my identity!!! Having those conversations and the things that were happening would eventually lead one to a heartbreak. Such a heartbreak could cause you to miss who you are, because it will cause you to begin to behave as someone who you know you're not. It will cause you to act out of character. The mind of a man would have you believe that you were wrong when all the time you were right however you were being blinded by the love that wasn't love. The manipulation and control of man was so intense if things were wrong and I knew they were I would somehow make myself believe the wrong was right because I thought it was love, it was just that they loved what they saw. They were never designed to love me; they weren't there for that purpose.

Up close I'm reminded when the lust was at its highest, trying to appear as if it was love. One evening it showed itself when I saw what should have been care and concern with a gentleman and his sister. He was an associate who became a friend, who then became someone of different character. He passed her something and instantly I had a freeze moment. What he passed her didn't help her in the addiction she was already in. I thought to myself If he dealt with his sister in such away and not cared about her well-being, then who was I? Would one day he try to pass me off something? I knew I needed to get away from that quick!! Although, the material things cars, clothes, gold and money all looked very good however it just wouldn't leave my mind that one day somehow that could be me. I desired to be loved, because, if nothing else, I always knew my worth. This was because my parents had made sure that we knew that. Sometimes when lust shows up before love, you tend to open yourself up and allow all kinds of toxins, hurt, pain, abandonment issues, lust, deceit, deception, insecurities etc. to come in. This was one time when I thought it was love that came in my life, but I finally realized that love doesn't hurt, nor does it cause pain and that lust only cares about self-satisfaction and how it can benefit. Unfortunately, people live a life of this because they never get healed from what has happened in their lives. It left me feeling empty, as if I had wasted my time. My emotions and intelligence were being tampered with. It might have had something to do with my age back then. I guess my mental capacity at that age was too much for him. Still not exactly sure why I almost allowed it to affect me so much, I feel sometimes the desire of wanting to be loved and wanted could have you in a place of settling for less. It's when you get in such times as this when you can identify what it means to be loved but not loved. It's critical that you take control of your life at this very moment and accept the reality of what it is like being loved but not loved. I am thankful today that

I had the strength to get away from it. All the glitter, game and fame couldn't keep me bound. The drugs and alcohol were in my neighborhood and in some extremely near places to me. Witnessing how these things destroyed people I decided to stay away from its people who engaged in it. That's not to say that I never had a drink!!! In fact, I had plenty of those!!! My favorite two were Harvey Bristol Cream and Peach Schnapps. I remember my fingers getting burned by what they called a "roach." It was the smallest piece of a joint … marijuana, I am cracking up!! it was passed to me, burned my fingers, and fell out of my hands—never made it to my lips.

However, I had an addiction—trying to figure out myself. I craved to know and understand who I was. I knew all the emotional abuse, lies, betrayal, manipulation that were happening to me was because of those who didn't know how to love me. You must take notice of when its lust and not love very early, if you do not, you will eventually bring yourself to a very difficult place of battling YOU in the mind. Battling within yourself trying to figure out (you), this person who's acting out of character. You must understand that people who were never loved or never knew how to receive love will never be able to pour love into you. You must embrace love on your own through self-love. I began to realize that I was expecting something that was never intended to be given to me. I was subconsciously attracting the attention of people who didn't know what love was. Neither did they know what it was, nor did they know how to. Because they didn't know how to love, they didn't know how to love me. The only love (lust) they had was hidden in their intentions, which was to get what they saw and wanted. You want people to not only love what they see, that is, your body but also to love you as a person. My desire was to be loved!! Once I understood the repeated cycle of people loving what they saw and not able to love me as a person. I came to a place of understanding. I was sure of one thing: Love doesn't make you become who you're not. It enhances you to become who you are destined to be.

Suddenly, a dramatic change happened. I felt like God allowed me to experience so much within these two years. I almost thought that I was twenty-five and thirty at the age of seventeen and eighteen. I think of it now and always give God all the glory and all the praise, because He allowed me to experience some things in those two years that caused so much hurt that could have left me broken. Brokenness can cause you to struggle for years and never embrace happiness. When your identity is attacked if you're not careful, then it can lead you to a place of having low self-esteem and never evolve into the person you're created to be.

In my senior year of high school, I was privileged to leave school and go for a co-op position in printing. I was employed at the age of seventeen, with a paycheck. I was positioned for a level of responsibility and independence. I had watched my mother and father take care of us. I knew what it meant to have a paycheck; I knew what it meant to have an income; and I knew what it meant to be independent. At a very young age, I took advantage of it. Yes! My own independence I began to do things on my own and giving myself things, I desired to have. I began to investigate what I was seeing. I started to see myself as a beautiful, Black young woman who knew her worth. I was beginning to see myself as an independent girl, reaching for the stars—a place where I could love myself and did not have to worry about being loved and not loved.

I moved away from my mother and father to living on my own with my sister and my niece. My mother released her property to us for us to begin using all of what we learned from home. The same home where my grandfather instilled so much of love and wisdom in me!! It was during this time that I really began to embrace my identity. Being away from my mom and dad at that age, I felt like I was still on the step. I say this because I felt like although I was off the step, I still had the step mentality being limited in what I wanted to do. Not being able to embrace the things that were in my surroundings, I eventually came out of that mindset. I was forced to change jobs after I was injured carrying a case of paper at the printing company I had been working at since the beginning of my senior year of high school. It brought about a new chapter in my life. In life, the end of a thing means the beginning of something greater. I never knew that going through these trying seasons of my life would bring out the very best in me. As an adult, my father always said, "It is what it is, and it's going to be what's it's going to be." Although he never explained his meaning of the statement, I came to this conclusion that if you're able to make change about your situation despite what it looks like, you must take authority in it, because at the end of the day it's left up to you (me) to either accept it or reject it. If it's not beneficial to you, you must be in a place of being okay to acknowledge that and trust God. Allow the Lord to order your footsteps and be willing to take the steps.

Understanding that love is a word that goes deep into our souls, I think about the time when Jesus came down to earth, and how His identity was in question. He went through so many things down here to show and prove His Father's love. I wonder if Jesus ever thought about being loved but not loved! How often do we think about how He might have thought or felt? Was He loved for the miracles and the power He possessed? Or was he loved for who He was? One of the awesome things about Jesus, despite what the conditions were, was that He maintained His integrity and His character. He came down because of love and kept going even after being denied.

You may be in a place today where you may be questioning the love someone has for you or the love you have for someone. I would encourage you to stop for a moment and think about the love that Jesus has for you. As for me this is the greatest love story, I've ever been in. Jesus came down because there was a purpose for His coming. Remember, when Jesus laid down His life? Scripture says.... Greater love has no one than this that he lay down his life for his friends. No matter what's going on in your life, that's the love that will bring healing and deliverance to you if you embrace it. His love is not like that of a man, but it is unconditional love. He knows about all the pain and disappointments you have encountered throughout this life.

Deep hurt and lust must be dealt with from the root. How many relationships do we see torn apart because of this once it has been exposed? Both men and women can be affected by this. It leads to chains of bondage in people's lives. In each of those chains, each link holds something that has the potential to destroy you. Especially when one of the links has been identified as a soul tie, a powerful emotional bond to another person, very damaging. Forcing one not to be able to break free. It has you wrapped up—wrapped up in your mind! That's where the enemy puts a double chain it's a stronger force to keep a person in bondage. You try to figure out why you feel like you're being controlled. It's because you have opened your entire soul and allowed one to come in and woo you!! If you're not careful, that thing would try to tell you when to eat and when to sleep. Wrapped up in your heart … that's where the emotions take over. Your mind and your heart are telling you to leave, and your flesh is warring against them and telling you to stay.

*Loved but not loved* is a very emotional state. If you're feeling drained even after having a full night's sleep and a solid plate to eat, then know that chances are because you're being emotionally drained. I would encourage you to get to the altar, cry out for deliverance, and loosen up from the bonds of your soul tie of loved but not LOVED.

# CHAPTER 5

## Heard A Voice

As a little girl, while trying to figure out the voice when I heard it, I was thinking to myself and asking questions like: *Who was it or what is it?* As I journeyed through life as a teenager, I often heard the voice in the middle of the night, sometimes early in the morning—still not being able to discern what it was or who it was. I began to hear the voice in my dreams. In one dream, not only did I hear the voice but also heard it call my name!!! I remember jumping up out of my sleep to see if someone was calling me. As I looked down my steps, I realized there was no one in the house but me.

I heard it the most during quiet times of the day. I think about the song "Hush hush, somebody's calling my name!!!" There were many times in my life, I begin to hear the voice more frequently. I would hear it even while walking the halls of school—always thinking that someone was calling my name. I wasn't popular in school, so that was a very rare possibility. And I was never called by my first name. My dear friend, Mar, had started calling me by my last name "Hellams." Hence, before I knew it, everyone else had begun addressing me by that name even the teachers!! So, to hear "Maryann" was surprising.

When I joined our high school gospel choir, we would go out singing across the city and sometimes out of state. I began to hear the voice repeatedly, not knowing what it was or who it was. Whom I didn't know then but know now is the Holy Spirit would rest upon me. After graduating high school, I didn't pay much attention to the voice anymore. I was finally able to go out and get off the top steps of my home!!!! The last thing I wanted to do was listen to anyone tell me what to do and what I couldn't do. Although deciding within myself and saying to myself that I wasn't listening to the voice anymore, I believe the voice never stop speaking to me.

I remember one summer evening when I was getting dressed to go out, I heard the voice whisper, "Be watchful." I didn't really pay too much attention to it until later that night. My cousin T and I were out with a few of her friends. We were down on South Street in Philadelphia when a dark-colored car pulled up alongside us. The occupants were trying to get our attention to have a conversation. One of my cousin's girlfriends responded saying keep it moving not interested!! Not our taste.... the guy sitting in the back of the vehicle was offended, he pulled out what appeared to be a weapon. I remember us running down that dark street. I was grateful because earlier that evening the voice had told me to be watchful.

There were many other times when I heard the voice. As I got older, I started paying attention, however, I wasn't acknowledging it. As time and life went on, things began to happen. Anytime I was facing any difficult situations I always heard the voice instructing me.

I finally realized that it was the voice of the Lord one night when I was getting dressed for a cabaret. These were the parties when the host would sell tickets for you to get in the venue. Everybody would come and we would get together, laugh, and dance the night away!!! There would be plenty of food and drinks. On this night, as I was getting dressed, my radio was tuned into 105.3! Suddenly something unusual happened!! A song was played that CHANGED my life!!! Who would have ever thought a gospel song would be played on an R&B station!! When I listened to this song, tears began to stream down my face.

After listening to the song, I heard my name being called again that night a little while later!!! And, in response, I said "yes" to the Lord, and it was a complete "yes"!!! The more the intensity of my yes, the more I began to listen to the voice. I knew that this voice was for me, and not against me. The voice gradually began to tell me that I needed to change my walk and my talk. I no longer needed to do the things that I was doing; He was my Creator, and I was supposed to give my life to Him. He began to tell me to read the "Word of God" to finish our conversation. This led me to picking up the Holy Bible and reading it.

I began to see the reason for His calling. Yes, it opened my heart. Jesus began to take out the things that were in my heart. He began to comfort me, heal my heart from all the hurt and pain that was caused by people which left me heartbroken. The more I said "yes," the deeper my relationship with him went. My desire to want to be in His presence grew stronger.

I was learning how to become that yielded vessel to do whatever He told me to do. Now that I learned who the voice was, I humbled myself to listen and obey it. Now I truly understand when Jesus said that my sheep know my voice and a stranger they will not follow. I saw my life change; the things of the world began to be stripped off me. No longer did I have the desire for partying, drinking, the bling and things!!! He began to show me my life from a higher perspective different part of my life began to flash before me. No longer were the cares of the world allowed to rest upon me, because I heard the voice of God.

My yes was intensified; I knew my yes to the Lord was beyond this world. My yes went into the Heaven!!!! One vision He showed me was spreading the message of the Gospel. When He began to show me this vision, it required a lot of preparation. The main part of my preparation was that I had to let go of the thing the world chooses which was sin. He began to equip me with His Word. He began to show me that He has given me gifts of healing, discerning of spirits, and that of prophecy. It took time for me to digest these things.

One thing I know is that I had to continue listening to the voice who had called me. I couldn't do things on my own anymore. I had the Lord in my life. I was blessed by Him for being my Savior. He showed me how I allowed him to be Lord!!!! Yes, He is the Lord however I wasn't acknowledging Him nor was I allowing Him to be my Lord. That meant that no matter what came my way,

I had to depend on Him—the one who was calling me. I had to trust Him, I had to believe Him, I had to know Him, I had to breathe Him, and I had to obey Him. I had to GO when He says GO and STOP when He says STOP!! I realized that there were going to be trials and tribulations in my life; there were going to be temptations; there were going to be things that would try to get me off course, and there were going to be things to try to get me away from my purpose.

He took me through the process!!! I had to *Digest the process!!!* I had to understand and accept the fact that my existence was no more about Maryann but about His command!!! I gave myself away!!! The voice said to me, "You're being constrained because you're in this world but not of it." One of the things He began to strip out of my life was alcohol. He said I should no longer have strong drinks, not even wine!! It has been twenty-seven years since I had any type of alcohol. These were the instructions for me. Therefore, you must make sure that you not only hear the voice but also know it. He knows who you are and who He created you to be. He knows why He doesn't want me to consume any kind of alcohol.

Around the very beginning, I used to think about it: *Not just a little wine????* Then I would often hear people when they would say, Jesus turned water into wine. Yes, He did! That was a miracle!! I look at this as a miracle in my life when He took away the desire for His glory. When you hear the voice, you don't know what's going to come with the stripping away, which turns out to be anything that will hinder you from doing His will and serving Him. All you can do is YIELD!!! Take a deep breath and focus on your YES. You know the stripping is for a purpose.

I think about the Book of Samuel in the Bible. I would say to you today, "Listen to the voice and know who's calling you. Know that you're being called for a purpose!! He's calling us from a world of sin!! The purpose of His calling is that we will one day reign with Him. When you become that *YIELDED VESSEL*, then you embrace your identity.

The thought of being a teacher had left me for a few years. I believe it was around the time when I had left my parents' home and had got a decent job. This was one of the times when I heard the voice again. I began to connect with the voice; every time it spoke! I remember hearing the voice for many days on Spring Garden Street. After learning it was the voice of God. I began to talk to Him more.

One day I came home early from my office. My daughter and son were still in school. My husband was still at work. I lay across my bed and heard the voice call my name. However, this time it was different from the other times. As I reflect on this moment I'm reminded when the Lord called Samuel. He heard his name being called and thought that it was his earthly father calling him. I often go back to that scripture, because that's exactly how I heard my name being called. However, there was no one home for me to ask if they were calling me. It often happens this way. I'm always in the house or a room by myself and hear the voice. I still looked around to see if there was someone.

I believe today that God allowed me to always be alone when He spoke to me so that I could know that it was really Him. I'm so forever grateful for hearing that voice. The voice told me how to be a mother, a wife, a friend, and a teacher. The word "teacher" takes my memory back to the time when it was said to me, that one day I will be a teacher. After hearing the voice call my name on this day, I got up and did something different this time: I called my mother-in-law, who is now home to be with the Lord.

As I spoke to her, I began to share my dreams with her. She asked me to join her at church on Sunday. I told her that I will not be able to join her on that Sunday, but that I will go with her soon. As the weeks went on, her Pastor, the late Pastor W. M, began asking me to visit the Church. I believe that my mother-in-law had shared our telephone conversations with him. I was more and more in tune with this voice now. I started sharing more and more with her about what I was hearing. That was truly the beginning of a beautiful spiritual relationship. I remember asking her for scriptures to read and study. I desired to learn about the person who was speaking to me.

I didn't go to church, looking for anything or anybody. I went seeking Jesus Christ. By then I knew enough about Him to know it was Him whom I needed! I knew that I had to put Jesus first. I went back and repented. Although I had given my life to Jesus when I was fourteen years old, I knew how important it was to *REPENT!!* I wasn't focused on the Lord from the age of sixteen through twenty, the hardest time was between 18 and 20 I knew I was in a backslidden state.... This condition occurs when you turn back to the world and away from Jesus. Those two years were very fast; so much happened.

I thank God that by the end of the age nineteen my husband came into my life. As time went on, I started going back to Church. I started praying more and listening for the Lord's voice more. I knew that something had shifted in my life. The Lord's voice had become stronger, and I was growing stronger. He began to tell me who I was. I didn't understand what He was telling me, but I always remembered the one thing that was said to me: I will be a teacher. The Lord would speak to me. I was made uncomfortable in places where I wanted to be, but which weren't fit for me. All I could do was follow what I was hearing. I could no longer drink my wine or go out to parties. The voice I heard was constantly speaking to me now. It was telling me that I needed to put Him first for me to be the mother, wife, friend, daughter, and teacher I was created and called to be.

I recognized this was the voice that was calling me when I used to play with the tops, lay paper down, and pretend to be a teacher. The same way I wanted the students to pay attention to me when I called their name or spoke to them was the same sternness, was the same way I heard the Lord's voice speaking to me. He wasn't speaking to my flesh, because my flesh was in a mess. My flesh would not listen; I was rejecting it, not realizing that it was me disobeying the voice of God. I remember being convicted in my heart. I repented for I knew this was the right thing to do!!!

Anytime the voice spoke to my spirit, I had to stop doing whatever I was doing. Some of the hardest things I battled with was when the voice told me that I could no longer go to certain places. I had to trust in the Lord and not lean on my own understanding. I was walking out when the scripture said, "Come from among them and be separated." I really didn't understand the separation at the time, which sometimes left me confused and lonely.

Was I being separated because I was loved but not loved? Or because I was called strange? I was trying to process all these things happening in my life without questioning. Finally, I was able to understand it was the Lord who told me that I had to be separated and why my life depended on it. While accepting the fact that all the friends I had, whom I loved dearly were no longer to be found, to talk to, or to go out with. It was like everybody around me just separated themselves, or perhaps the voice separated me from them.

I often think about the friends I had even to this day, as I'm writing. There were only a few friends and associates. Rather than talking about what was happening or what was going on, I would often talk with the Lord about how I was feeling, which I used to keep to myself otherwise. I knew that when I would find myself in deep thought about it the Lord would call me back from that place. He would pull me in and comfort me. I got stronger and better. I began going to church. I wasn't going to church to hear the choir sing, to fellowship, or to go to other churches on trips, I went to seek after the voice that was calling me.

I remember getting my children ready for Church when I heard the voice through a song. One night, while getting dressed to go out to a club, I heard this song and began to hear the voice, and that's when my life changed forever!! I no longer was able to be in the church and in the world, too. I made a 360-degree turn to my Lord and Savior Jesus Christ and I've been serving him, worshiping him, and praising him since November of 1998!

Wow! As the voice continued to become stronger, I became stronger in accepting the things that were happening in my life. Now I was not only hearing the voice but also listening to and obeying the voice. As I'm listening, it's leading, directing, and guiding me. As I was being led, guided, and directed, He was ordering my footsteps. I didn't understand it all, however, all I knew is that I wanted the voice and the only way I could connect with that voice was that I had to make sure that it was nothing that came before it.

My life was changing! WOW!! Listening to the voice I desired more of Him that was speaking to me, any time, we were having two services at the Church I would make sure I was in both. I begin to say I need this! I need this! Because it was making a difference in my life. It was starting to show me who I really was. The voice began to speak to me about my husband, not just on one occasion, but several times. I paid attention, and it spoke to me and told me to begin to pray for my husband, and not for my selfish reasons. I was to pray for my husband so that my husband would give his life back to Christ.

I began to pray and understand that if I was going to be a light, I needed to make sure that my husband and my children saw it first. I began to pray for my husband, and the voice let me know that my husband wasn't far from Him. He wasn't far from Him mentally or in his heart. After knowing this, I no longer prayed to ask God to send him to Church to help me with the babies. I no longer wanted God to send him to Church just so he could be sitting next to me. I began to pray earnestly that he would give his life back to our Lord and Savior Jesus Christ.

As I listened to the voice, not only did it begin to get intense, but it also made me nervous. I didn't realize at the time the voice was beginning to prepare me for what was getting ready to happen in my life. Our Church was having a full week of service. Bishop from Conway South Carolina came up and hosted the first night. I can say REVIVAL!!! I didn't want to miss it. My husband wanted me to make a pot of rice with the rest of the dinner, and I told him, "No, you have to make it…. I'm running late!!!" Little did I know it was going to be my first encounter with the voice, speaking through His prophet.

When I arrived at Church, service was beginning. I was extremely excited that we had an out-of-state preacher to deliver the Word. My stomach seemed to have had butterflies while sitting in the sanctuary. All I knew was that the Lord was going to give me a word!!!! I'm spiritually hungry; I've been listening to this voice and knew that there was more! And the Lord sent it through this little five-foot-one prophet. He stood up and began to minister, and the Holy Spirit fell on him while he began to say, "There's somebody here who did not obey the voice of the Lord!!!" He looked and looked and looked again. I'll never forget it. My baby girl was sitting off to the left side of me while my son was in his car seat, sitting with my mother-in-law. He said, "To you in the navy-blue suit, why didn't you make that pot of rice for your husband before you left home? Charity begins at home!!!" I could have passed out!!!

Instantly I was able to understand the connection, the voice of the Holy Spirit was speaking to me and was now speaking to me through his Prophet. I lifted my hands and tears began to fall. I cried and asked the Lord to forgive me. I came home and apologized to my husband. From that time, I never went to church before making sure that dinner was made. I became a yielded vessel yearning and obeying.

In June of 2000, my life took a turn. I was called into the pastor's study. I was accompanied by our Pastor Elder Deacon Secretary and Mother of our Church. The way everyone was sitting around, I thought I was in some trouble…. A few minutes later, the prophet whom the Lord assigned at the time to our Church came in. He told me to have a seat and began speaking saying, "The Holy Spirit has been speaking to me about you. Now it's time for you to go forward in the gospel." I looked at him—confused, not understanding what all was happening. He continued, "Now is the time for you to go forward." Instantly I remembered when the Lord spoke to the disciples and He told them to go out into the hedges in highways and compel men and women, boys and girls to come. I never questioned anything, because the feeling that would come over me when the Holy Spirit was speaking fell on me very strongly this time. I was given instructions and told to go out and evangelize. I went into prayer, seeking the Lord. As I began to study the evangelist, I understood that I was going out to seek souls and share the Gospel of Jesus Christ. In sharing, I found myself teaching people His characteristics. I remember one Saturday afternoon going to my mother's home. Because the young people love her so much, they are always assembled around her porch. On this day, the teacher came out of me. I shared with them who Jesus was giving them a clearer understanding of who they were denying. I'll never forget this one precious young man who looked at me and said, "Now I understand, Maryann…. Later that summer, he gave his heart to the Lord. I watched him walk in his salvation over the years, and although he went through a season of struggling, he kept the Lord's name on his lips. He walked through his deliverance, and when he left this world, he left knowing Jesus Christ as his Lord and Savior!!

I went out seeking souls to be saved, telling everyone that I encountered about Jesus!! I saw my life change; my life was being rearranged. I began to have a hunger for souls. My faith assured me that if it was the will of the Lord, then if someone was sick, they could be healed. I KNEW that if someone was in bondage, they could be free; if someone was in sin, they could be saved; and if someone was dirty, they could be cleansed. I went out seeking those souls who were crying, hurting, in pain, depressed, downtrodden by the cares of life. I went telling everybody that Jesus is Lord, that no matter where they've been and what they've been through, Jesus is Lord and He's Savior. He would come in their heart if they let Him. I told them that if they allow Him to be the Lord, He will lead their life, He will guide them, He will speak to them, and He will make a change if they would allow him to save them from this wicked world! I told them if they were having trouble, He'll give them peace.

The zeal in my life during the beginning of my evangelism days was like body needs water. I could see the danger upon people's lives. I could see the need for salvation for more reasons than one!!! Introducing them to Jesus was my mission!! To see lives changed became my passion!! I knew it was possible for them, because it happened for me. Our Lord Jesus Christ is the God who is no respecter of persons. This means no matter who I went to, I told them about Jesus. I told them that if they would just lift their hands, repent, and ask the Lord for forgiveness, salvation belonged to them. Oh, my goodness! The hunger for souls continued to get more intense. Before I knew it, I was going throughout my family, telling everybody about Jesus. I was going throughout my neighborhood, telling everybody about Jesus! I started inviting them to our Church. The young people were looking for a way of escape. Many were trying to escape the pain that they were in. They were looking for healing, not realizing that they were even sick. I remember being asked to be the keynote speaker for a youth revival in Philadelphia. The Lord blessed everyone in attendance! Souls were saved and lives were changed instantly. That same year, there was a youth revival happening within the fellowship of Churches. During the service I was called to the front of the Church along with the youth and was awarded for being an outstanding youth director.

My faith allowed me to believe that *JESUS IS THE CONCLUSION TO ALL OF OUR CONFUSION*. Seeking souls to be saved and having a desire for lives to be changed—no matter what was going on in their life; whether they were broken or brokenhearted, blind, sick, or diseased—I knew that if we lifted the name of Jesus, He said that He would draw all men unto Him.

After spending time at our church on Huntington Park in Philadelphia, my hunger for souls was great. The devil saw my focus. He saw the Kingdom being built. He was upset and showed Himself. Many forces came to try to distract me and push me away from hearing the voice. I eventually left the fellowship, but I didn't leave God. Although I knew the devil was trying to destroy me, I had to remind him that I belonged to the Lord. I knew the Lord had His hands upon my life, and He had chosen me.

I didn't realize the Lord was allowing things to happen around me to lead me into my destiny. The Holy Spirit told me to not be a grasshopper. I asked, "A grasshopper?" The response was, "Yes, grasshoppers don't go jumping, don't hop from fellowship to fellowship! You get where you can hear me, where you can see me, where you can receive my word, and be the yielded vessel I'm calling you to be." At that time, the only place to which I felt led was my bedroom. Hence, my bedroom was where I went. I didn't go to any other Church. I didn't go talking about the past. I didn't talk about members of the fellowship. I didn't talk about what was going on. I didn't go talk about how the devil came through!! I understood that it was the devil, and his goal was not only to try to destroy me but also to bring me shame against the Church. I always kept in mind that the world was watching, even if they hadn't decided to follow Jesus. The things that the devil was doing, I took them to the pastor and the Lord in prayer. I went to my room, and I stayed there Sunday after Sunday. We must understand that when the Lord is leading us, it's very important that we obey! When He says, "Stand still," then that is what you must do!!! I realize that I didn't leave the building because of my own understanding, it was truly the Lord allowing some things to happen to bring a shift in my life. The events that followed shortly thereafter were proof that it was Him who was moving me. Again, the Lord saved me from destruction!

I remember one day while I was sitting, listening to one of the gospel television networks and watching the different preachers. My spirit and soul were being filled, my mind was being regulated, and my heart was getting fixed. Sitting still allowing the Lord to order my footsteps and not running and missing the restoration and refreshing that I needed. While sitting I began to hear the voice again, and the voice said, *"A New Walk with Christ."* Weeks went by, and I heard again, *"A New Walk with Christ"*; this time the voice told me to write it down. I wrote it down, not understanding what it meant at the time when the scripture said write the vision. I didn't know that it was a vision. I just thought that my walk was going to get better.

I received a phone call on a Monday evening. It was the voice of my mother-in-law, the late Elder Louise Nathaniel and Bishop P. E. J. They had a conversation with me, and during the conversation, the bishop said to me, "Your mother wants to talk to you about something." I knew my mother-in-law had started a Church prior to me meeting my husband. I knew that she was a minister of the gospel. I knew there was an anointing upon her life. And I knew that she was powerful. However, what I didn't know was that the Lord was going to use her to pull me into my destiny. She began to talk about how she wanted to go back and start the ministry work, all over again. She wanted to do what the Lord had called her to do. The Holy Spirit begun to speak to her. One of the things she said which I laugh to this day was that I was the to-be pastor, and she would be the overseer. I said, "NO, I will do whatever I need to do to assist you in the work of the ministry. You're the pastor, and you should go back into the vineyard as the pastor." Then she began to talk while the bishop, and I listened. I said, "Bishop, she's the pastor. I will help her in whatever needs to be done.

I'll make flyers, I'll go around in the neighborhood to invite, I'll go witness, I'll set up whatever she needs me to do." I'll do it. Again, I heard the voice say, "*A New Walk with Christ.*" It's very important that we humble ourselves and be sure that we are in alignment with the will of the Lord and not eager for a position or a title, but that we know the CALL of GOD in and for our lives.

A month later, we began having services in the living room and dining room of her home. The vision that God had given to her was awakened. Not knowing that I was a part of the vision from the very first time that it was birthed, she didn't know me, but God knew our destiny!! We started having services United Fellowship Deliverance Church was lifted to the Heaven and the Lord blessed it! From the living room to sharing space with another Church from there to my sister Claresa's basement.

During the time of those three moves my mother-in-love who became my pastor became ill and went home to be with the Lord September 7th, 2005, 10 days before my birthday!!! She and I shared many ministry moments which were teachable moments. It was like she was pouring everything in me that was needed. Sometimes I didn't understand why she was operating the way she was however I knew her relationship with the Lord meant everything to her and her biggest thing was that she obeyed Him. She left me with instructions, part of the instructions was to carry on the vision.

Her final message she preached to the congregation was I'm pressing on!! Y'all keep PRESSING!! A New Walk with Christ spoke loudly. I now fully understood what was happening. The voice of the Holy Spirit leading, guiding and directing me. I never thought about the church, ministry, nor about what would happen or what should happen. I had peace in my spirit. My heart was hurting because my husband and my children were hurting. And although I was hurting, I had to cover my hurt up and be strong for my husband and children. My focus was on my family.

I shared with Apostle J. who was then Mother J. that the voice had spoken in my heart, "A New Walk with Christ." I did not want to step up as a pastor in the same month, the next month, or the following month. I wanted to do it in the month she and I first stood together and began working in the ministry in the vineyard together in December 2002. The voice spoke to me and said a new walk with Christ, and this is the time that it manifested itself.

I became the pastor of *United Fellowship Deliverance Church*. I will say to you today, "Listen to the voice and know the voice who's calling your name. Know that you are created for a purpose. I began to get to know who was calling my name. The devil will try to stop you from reaching your destiny and purpose. Many other voices will call your name!!! It could be a voice of drugs, alcohol gambling, whoremongering—whatever voice calls you, be certain that you listen very carefully! KNOW THE VOICE!!!"

I often think about the incident when Samuel lay down to sleep and the voice of the Lord called him. He called him three times. Each time He called; Samuel responded to his earthly father. His father told him that it was not him, and he told him to go back and lie down. The third time his earthly father said to him, "If you hear Him call again, you respond by saying, 'Speak Lord, for your servant heareth.'" Samuel went to lie back down and heard the voice of God call him again. He answered, "Speak Lord, your servant heareth!!!!"

Sometimes in our lives and our spiritual walk, we can become confused. Samuel was confused by the voice; however, he obeyed his earthly father's voice by lying down and listening to the voice. Don't be distracted; listen closely. Recognize the voice; yield to the voice that's calling you. It's calling you with a purpose and a destiny. Block out all the other voices that are calling you. Remember they are causing distractions because they don't want you to hear what God has for you to hear. Most of the times, we try to figure out our path in life by listening to what others have to say about us, what their opinions are about what we should do, where we should go, what we should eat, and what we should drink. It takes us away from listening to our creator, the one who tells us what's best for us. The one who calls our name, so that we can embrace our identity.

Have you ever been somewhere in a crowd or in the mall, shopping, or walking around in your neighborhood or walking down the street when suddenly you hear someone call your name? Have you then turned around and said, "Oh! I thought I heard somebody calling me."? What if those were the times when the Lord was calling your name? In those moments, when He called your name, you stopped and looked around to see who it was, but you didn't see anybody. Sometimes He calls us to stop us from going down the wrong road or listening to the wrong people. Remember, when you hear your name called out and you look around only to find no one there, then you should take a moment to say, "Speak Lord, your servant heareth." Don't miss the call, because then you can miss out on your calling and purpose in life.

When you acknowledge the voice, humble yourself repent and answer. Remain at the feet of Jesus and obey Him!!

# CHAPTER 6
## Called By God

A moment in my life that I didn't take lightly or for granted was the moment I was called by God. It's likened when you were a child, and your parents called your name. You would make haste to come, if you didn't go as quick as they called your name there was a consequence behind your delay. I often think about being called by God. I have come to a place of knowing that when it happened in my life, my life no longer remained my own. I became a yielded vessel. That's truly when I realized that I was being called by God.

When I sit and think about being called by God, I think about the time when God had called Moses up to the mountaintop, where he had witnessed a burning bush, and the fire would never go out. As Moses got up to that place, he was in the presence of the Lord. The Lord Our God our Father told him to take off his shoes, for the place where he was standing was Holy Ground. It was there in that place where God began to speak to Moses and give him instructions.

It's important for us to know that when God calls us, He not only gives us instructions but also equips us for the call. I never questioned the call of God on my life. I just always wondered why He chose me. How does that sound? It's funny, because I never questioned Him, but I struggled thinking, *why me?* I struggled for many years, because I often wondered "why," never questioning God, but just questioning myself. Because knowing that He, being the creator of the universe, makes no mistakes. He has proven to me several times that it was He who was calling me. I acknowledged the call of God in my life at the age of twenty-four, however, I knew that there was a call ten years prior, when I was fourteen years of age, but when I just didn't understand it. During this time in my life, I was very emotional. During my junior high school year, my grandfather became very ill. I watched the strong powerful intelligent man who loved, encouraged and taught me become very weak and fragile. He was a very tall man, and his hands were huge!! You wouldn't want to get hit by those hands!!! Even in his sickness, I watched him to continue to remain standing tall in his faith in the Lord. He was never a quitter!! I know that part of him was sown deep in my roots!!

His illness did not last long. I believe that he knew about it long before he shared this news with us. Weeks and months flew by!! I remember trying to hold on to every second that we had! When my grandfather went home to be with the Lord, it was the first time when I watched someone live out their final days. Watching my mother grieve was the hardest. During that time, I was trying to understand why, at such a young age, I was able to understand everything that was happening—desiring to stand as if I was an adult.

There were days when I would come home from school and not think about homework. I was thinking about washing him up to make sure that he was comfortable. I remember rubbing his back one-night crying, he asked me "Why are you rubbing my back? I replied, "Because I am rubbing the cancer away!!" Being a child, I didn't understand what I was saying at the time. I often think about that, and how, even then, the Lord was showing me: I had enough faith to know that if I laid hands on the sick, they would be healed.

I always question: Why did my grandfather call me to the table to tell a four-teen-year-old that he had cancer and was sick. Why did he tell me first when he had so many adult children? He could have called them and shared it with them. That was one of the things that was brought to my attention at a very young age—that I was being told something very strong, heavy, and painful. I knew from that experience that the Lord would not put more on me than I could bear.

In life you take a different turn to walk a different walk. You must be more, take more, go through a little bit more, digest more, and sit alone more.

When there's a call on your life, you're being separated from the world. In fact, you are already separated, but you don't understand the separation. I tried to push through the separation and try to be a teenager. Learning that my life was different from the age of two, I began to understand that I couldn't do what everyone else was doing. The Word of God tells us we are in the world but not of the world.

When I tried to do what everybody was doing, it never was well with me, it just wasn't right and turned out to be an embarrassment. Why? Because I didn't fit in, I kept trying to push, not knowing and understanding that there was a call on my life. I just had to push through the age of fourteen, fifteen, and sixteen, struggling with my identity. Pushing against what was calling me, I tried to fight it. I tried not to be who I was called to be. I started doing things other children and teenagers were doing. Started trying to talk like everybody else, trying to walk like everybody else, but again not knowing that there was a call and not understanding the call. I dealt with separation, loneliness, identity crisis, and struggle. The struggle of desiring just to be able to have fun, not realizing the fun that I wanted to be a part of was the fun that was causing a lot of dark days for people.

Knowing and accepting that I was being called from that place so that I could be positioned to call people from that place!!! Loneliness was the hardest part, because I suffered a lot because I was said to be different. Being called different or special caused a lot of enviousness and jealousy. I struggled with that, because I didn't understand what it was. I didn't understand why people who I thought loved me did not actually love me; they loved me, but they didn't love me!!!! Yeah, that's a twist right there. You can be loved by somebody because of the relationship status, but then it can become difficult for them to show their love, once they discover who you are … it's not them, it's the thing that's on the inside of them that's trying to keep them from getting to know the love that's on the inside of you—a love that will be used to speak to them and to

**49**

keep them from the dark place. Wow coming into the age and understanding the call, moving forward it got a little deeper. Now I couldn't be the wife and mother who I thought I was going to be. I thought I would have a family and remain in the world. Now, I had to understand how the Lord had designed my life to be. Being called by Him and gifted to be a wife and a mother.

The call was going to require me to spend quite time with God, for which I had to give up some dinners, some of my personal time, some intimate time with my husband, and some time with children, I had to learn how to balance. I had to be there for other families; for the sick in the hospital; for death, births, and marriages; and for counseling. So, the call may require you to sacrifice. I began going back to that same place of trying to understand why I was called. Then the voice whispered and said, "You were called because I created you. I'm going to redeem the time. I'm going to fill the void. I assure you that your husband and your children are good." He assured me that my home was blessed.

It was at this very moment when I accepted my call and had the assurance from God that everything will be good. My children and husband were good. Then I was able to move forward in the call of God, knowing He's the Creator and He had called me. Because He had called and created me, I had to be that yielded vessel to answer Him. I had to answer the call like Moses had answered, even though when Moses got before God, he began talking to God and giving Him a reason why he was not qualified. He talked to God about his speech, and God began to tell him, "I'm going to send your brother Aaron and he will speak for you.

In life, you will come to a place of realizing that when God called you, he was going to empty you out. To empty out means that you must empty out your feelings and emotions to accept the call. Understanding that you're human and sometimes the flesh doesn't want the flesh to pray, you will have to pray for those who despitefully use you. The flesh doesn't want you to go and be with people who have stabbed you in your back. The flesh doesn't want you to be with friends who have betrayed you. Your flesh doesn't want you to be who God has called you to be. When your flesh wants to fight against your spirit, remember the Lord's voice. I was victorious every time, because all I focused on was hearing the Holy Spirit saying, "I'm calling you; I'm calling you with a purpose." I never fully understood how to be a yielding vessel until He began to show me why it was important that I become one and what was coming along with being one. A Complete work had to be done in me and through me.

When He dealt with me, one of the very first things were my emotions. To be a yielded vessel, that area of your life must be dealt with. It allowed me to gain control of my flesh. Being stripped of your emotions doesn't mean your feelings and concerns go unnoticed, it simply means your emotions will not be allowed to cause you to act in any other way than how the one who called you to act. The God we love and serve simply puts us on the potter's wheel and spins and shapes us into that yielded vessel. The spinning doesn't feel good. The anointing is over your very life to cover and protect you. The anointing heals those wounds. It strengthens you and makes you better instead of bitter. It makes you whole instead of broken. It takes you out of the place of being caught up in your mind.

The thoughts in your mind sometimes try to overpower you. The fights in your mind can cause fights in your heart. To be a yielded vessel, your heart should be in the right place, free from hurt pain unforgiveness anything that's not like the character of God. Scripture tells us if we keep our mind focused on the Lord, He will keep us in the perfect peace. Called by God sometimes seems chaotic, because the enemy would try to make a lot of noise to distract you from the call. Confusion would have its way of showing up as well. You ask the question, "Why me??" And although you're saying, "Why me?" it sounds strange, because though you are questioning God, you're questioning yourself.

While going through this season, I came to realize that God is not the author of confusion. I understood what was happening while I was spinning on the potter's wheel—I found myself in an identity crisis. You must walk through all the frustration, all the hurt, all the pain, all the betrayal, and all the isolation. While trying to figure out why I was back at this place of questioning who I was again, I realized that it was necessary for me to say yes from deep within. I know that I was being called, I was different, I was in this world but not of this world, I had an assignment in my life, and my life had a purpose. You never give that deep yes until you begin to experience the EXPERIENCE.

Something deep down on the inside of you begins to build your yes!! This small, three-letter word "YES" goes past you pain, misunderstanding, confusion, doubt, and identity crisis. It goes past the fact that you are a mother, a wife, a daughter, a sister, a niece, or a cousin.

*Your YES becomes ETERNAL, not Internal.* It becomes eternal means it goes past the earth realm. It means nothing in this world could shake your YES. MY eternal yes put me to the place where I was walking with my eyes closed in spirit. I was walking by faith not by sight. My life is faith because of my faith. For some time, I was going through and processing the yes with my eyes closed. On some days, my eyes were closed, because of the things that I was seeing. I knew that I was being hated, but I still had the love. I knew that I was losing, but I knew that I was still winning. I knew that I was sick, but I knew that I was still healed. I knew that I was in bondage, but I knew still I was being free. I knew that I was broken, but I knew I was being made whole. *My life became my faith, and my faith became my life.*

I began setting my eyes on the things that were above. I remember confessing out of my mouth daily that I can do all things through Christ, who strengthens me. I began to look at the things above, and I began to hear the voice of God saying, "I gave you a gift of healing. Go to the hospital room, lay hands on the sick, and expect them to be healed. Go and lay hands on the mental and on those who were in bondage. When you believe past the internal and press into the eternal whatever you lay your hands upon so shall it be!

# CHAPTER 7

## Christ's Blood Intertwined With My Blood

In July 2015, I had just come back for our annual Women Worshiping at the Water Gathering and was sitting in my office when I experienced some pain in the lower extremity of my left-leg calf. The pain went on for about two days before I noticed that it was getting more intense while sitting. Finally, on the Friday afternoon that week, I said to my sister Claresa, "I can't take this pain anymore." We left the office early, around 4:35 p.m., heading over to Hahnemann Hospital that was located at the southwest corner of Broad and Vine streets. Our actual plans had changed. Earlier, we had planned to go to my mother's house to have some fish on that Friday.

When we arrived at the hospital, our visit went on for several hours for them to tell me that it was a muscle strain. I remember requesting them to do an x-ray or an ultrasound on my leg. I had experienced a pulled muscle before, but this was a different pain. This pain was more intense. Around 3:30 of Saturday morning, they discharged me. I came home to prepare for our women's ministry meeting that was set for that afternoon. I was able to get a little sleep. I woke up, but fell back to sleep, then woke up again. And this time, the Holy Spirit began to tell me that something more serious was going on in my leg. He had me grab my phone I went online, and I began looking up blood clots, not knowing that He was diagnosing me right in my bathroom.

I began to look up: what causes blood clot and what needed to be done to get it resolved. In my reading, I found out that blood clots could be deadly. Praying the whole time, I pushed myself throughout the day. I went to the church for the meeting. I had to have my leg up on the chair. I started feeling my pants getting a little tight. The pain was so bad that I had to end the meeting. I had to take the mother of the church and another member of the church home, but I couldn't drive that much. So, I drove to my house, and then I asked my husband to drop them home. When he left to take them home, I went up the stairs to prepare for my uncle's home-going service that evening. While getting ready, I started feeling heavy in my chest. By the time my husband got back home, my toes had started turning a little dark. I told my husband that I needed to go to the hospital.

I went back to the hospital and immediately requested them to perform an ultrasound!!! I told them I had just been there for almost twelve hours, only to be told that I had muscle strain. I told them that I believed it was more than a the diagnosis they gave me. I told them I believed that I had a blood clot, and that it was traveling. The triage nurse asked me if I suffered from blood clots, to which I said no. I informed her that I began researching it early this morning. When they took me to the triage room, the nurse began to check my pulse, my heart wasn't beating normally, so they immediately did an EKG (electro-cardiography), and all I heard was ultrasound stat!! They took me to the back and began to prepare me for the ultrasound. The ultrasound tech came in and did the ultrasound. It showed that I had a blood clot!!!! My husband was in the room with me. The pain!!!! Oh my!! My chest began to feel so heavy that I was losing my breath. The thought of the same hospital I was born in could have been the same hospital I might have taken my last breath in.

I began telling my husband that I needed to eat something. It felt like I was leaving here. He ordered some food. But when you're in the emergency room, they tell you that you can't have anything to eat or drink. The nurse came in to do my IV line and noticed that my husband had something to eat. She said, "Oh no, you can't have that." Immediately, I grabbed the onion ring that my husband had ordered out of the tray. It felt like when it hit my stomach, fire burned in my stomach it made me sit up I began to vomit. When I vomited a portion of the blood clot, the size of a plum, I remember dropping back.

When I woke up later that night, I was in a hospital room on the sixteenth floor of Hahnemann Hospital. I stayed in the hospital for almost two weeks after they ran several tests and discovered a few other things that were going on with me, some of which could have led to the possibility of the cause of the blood clot. They were never able to get to the bottom line of what caused it. Wow!!! Just thinking what if I would have pressed my way to my uncle's home-going service I might not would have made it out of the service!!! I just began to backtrack and think on some things that I had been doing. I had taken meat out of my diet for almost eight months and started eating more fruits, beans, and vegetables. I also did some extensive driving during that time. I was eating a lot of greenery and a lot of beans that, I learned, had high amounts of vitamin K. The vitamin K caused my blood to get thick.

The fact that I was doing a lot of driving was causing my blood not to flow much. I was diagnosed with what's called deep vein thrombosis. I was discharged having to take blood thinner. After being home for about a week. I had to go back to have my INR checked. When I went to have my INR check, it was at a 3.3. I was told by my doctor to skip the dose of the blood thinner that evening because my blood was too thin.

When I came back home from my appointment, my sisters Claresa and Carrie were with me. During this time, I couldn't go up the steps. I had to stay down on my first floor. Going up the steps would have triggered the blood clot to travel. When I came home, I felt the urge to go upstairs and use the restroom, it had been a while since I had been upstairs. I wanted to test the strength in my legs. My downstairs had become my bedroom and the restroom. Going up the steps, I took my time. I felt good while climbing up the steps. I remembered the time when I was going into the bathroom, while I was in the bathroom, and while I was coming out. However, as soon as I got to the top of the steps, everything went white.

The next thing I know was that I woke up in the nearby hospital. When they got me there, my blood count was down to two. My husband was immediately told that I was going to need a blood transfusion. I was bleeding on the inside; however, they couldn't find where. The blood thinners had caused my blood to thin out too much. The blood was ordered, which was lost twice while coming from the blood bank to the emergency room. I heard when the nurse notified the doctor that they couldn't locate the blood. I remember signing my consent form to accept the blood transfusion; however, by the time they got me to the fifth floor of the hospital, they indicated that my consent form had been lost!!!! At this point I got convinced that the devil was trying to kill me!

They couldn't find it, so they couldn't start the process of blood transfusion until they found the consent form. Currently, my blood count was getting lower. I remember asking the nurse, "Did they check down at the nurses' station? The transporter had everything on the clipboard when he brought me up. Maybe he stopped at the nurses' station and dropped it off." She said, "You know what, let me go down there and check." She went down to check the nurses' station, and there was the clipboard with all my information along with the consent form. She came back in, and I remember looking at the clock that read 3:13. It was thirteen minutes after my normal 3 a.m. prayer time.

I can't remember her name, but she was a short, sweet nurse. She couldn't find veins to start the blood transfusion and was working very hard to find a vein. She eventually said, "I really don't want to put it in your hand, but I'm going to have to, because I don't want the blood to start clotting; you already have a clot situation going on." I asked her to put it in my left hand, so that I would be able to use my right hand. I remember her putting the needle in my hand and looking at the clock that read 3:16. I was instantly reminded of John 3:16 for God so loved the world that he gave his only begotten son. That whosoever shall believe in him should not perish. I knew that I had the blood of Jesus Christ. I looked at my husband and said, "Gregory, you can go home now; you have to get up in a few hours."

I remembered that I had walked around for a whole year, not knowing why I was saying, "Lord, allow your blood to intertwine with my blood." It hit me in that room on the fifth floor that my spirit was crying out for the blood of Jesus for a whole year! My faith told me that it was that prayer that saved my life. The nurse started the blood to go through, and it was quite painful. I asked her to slow it down, and she said that she can slow it down just a little bit, because it had to go out by a certain time, because they didn't want the blood to clot. I remember her turning the IV down and the next thing I got to know was that I woke up when they were changing shifts and the blood was just getting out of the bag!! It was time for another bag; the new nurse came in and said, "I'm going to give you a break; you had a rough night." I said, "I don't remember the rough night at all. All I know is that the Holy Spirit was in the room with me, and I know that he gave me peace when I saw 3:16 on the clock, and then I just went to sleep. So, whatever my physical body was going through that they were able to see, I'm grateful, because I never experienced it. They saw something that I didn't see.

That's why my life is faith. I slept through it. During my stay at the hospital, I had several encounters with the Holy Spirit. I remember drifting off to sleep and having a dream of me running through grass. Oh my! The green was greener than green. As I looked out while running, there was a table with white linen and a tall figure standing on the other side of it.

The voice spoke instructing me to lie down. When I lay on the table, two hands appeared before me with a green substance. I was told to open my mouth, and it fed me the substance. I went out in the dream, and when I woke up, it told me to adorn myself in white. I said to myself, I'm in the hospital. Where am I going to get white from? And why do I need to be in white?? The next morning, the doctor came in and told me that they couldn't see where I was bleeding from, so they wanted to do a colonoscopy procedure.

This same day, my daughter came to the hospital with a bag of clothes for me. I just wasn't comfortable in the hospital gowns and had made up my mind that I wasn't going to look like I was in the hospital. When she came into the room, her smile was like the Sun that lit up my room. She climbed in my bed and put her head on my chest!!! I will never forget the charge of energy that came from my baby. Later that evening, I was able to check my bag to see what she had brought from home. As soon as I looked into the bag, there was the white!!!! Along with a brand-new pair of white socks!! Tears began to stream down my face!! I began to bless the Lord. I said, "Lord, this is the white you showed me!!" The Holy Spirit had instructed me to wear it down for the test the next morning!!

My nurse came in early to get me ready. She was preparing to give me the hospital gowns. I said, "Sorry, I can't wear that." She said, "For the test you're having, you will only need these two gowns." I said to her, "You can place them on my bed, and when I get down there, I'll put them on." I did just that, however, I was able to keep a portion of my white apparel on. When I woke up from the procedure, the doctor was standing over me and said, "Mrs. Nathaniel, you did great!! We didn't see any bleeding, and by the way, do you eat??" I said, "Yes, is there a concern?" She said, "No!! Whatever you're eating, continue eating, as your colon looks like a fourteen-year-old!!! You are healthy, Mrs. Nathaniel!!"

I was discharged from the hospital after three weeks. I was sent back home with a nurse. When I speak about my Lord and Savior Jesus Christ's blood inter-twining with my blood, it was that very thing that I held on to. I had that much faith to know that when his blood had intertwined with my blood, I would live and not die! I remember, lying downstairs on my couch one night during the time of the blood clot, because I couldn't go up the steps. The pain was so intense that it was taking my breath away. I had to stop the pain medication, because it was causing me to be constipated. That was bringing more pain.

I remember looking at my front door and the light from my bathroom illuminated down the steps from my stairways into my living room, and an image of a cross appeared on my door. I never really noticed the way my door was made and that there was a cross carved into it. I didn't want to wake my husband up, because he had to get up early for work. He never left my side, as I lay on our sofa, I remember him sleeping next to me on the floor. I remember crying as I listened to the worship music. Tears just ran down my face. I was trying to breathe and trying to divert my attention from the pain. All I remember saying to the Lord was, "Jesus, please take this pain away from me." I don't know when I drifted off to sleep.

Then I had a dream in which an angel came and stood over me, breathed into my nostrils, and began to speak to me. I don't know what he was saying in the dream, but after coming out of the dream, I knew the Holy Spirit taught me how to breathe through the pain. When I woke up the very next morning, I began to bless the Lord and thank him. During this time, my leg was filled with fluid, and it was almost double the size because of the blood clot. I was getting ready that morning to do my INR, and the Holy Spirit brought back my memory of how to breathe through the pain.

It was so intense that my heart was beating fast. When the nurse came, he began to talk to me and tell me the things we needed to do for the day. He looked at how I was breathing and said, "Mrs. Nathaniel, I don't like the way you're breathing." I said, "I'm breathing this way because of the pain." I didn't know how to share with him how the Holy Spirit had shown me the way to breathe through pain. I didn't want him to look at me like I was strange. But somehow, I felt that I needed to share it with him. It's my testimony!!!!! Ok witnessing time!!! I did just that. I told him the dream and how I was told how to breathe in between the pain. Well, as I suspected, he looked at me—confused. I asked him if he could just give me a minute to get myself together.

I heard a knock at the door. The nurse answered the door, and it was my brother Rickey. I was happy to see him. I felt the love and concern from him while he sat across from me. He had heard what the nurse was sharing with me and what was expected of me that day during the time of the visit and along with my therapist. I was told that I will be using the walker while in therapy. My therapy session consisted of me walking from my living room to my kitchen. On this day I said, "I'm not using the walker." I told my brother to close the walker up and put it in my dining room as I began to stand up.

As I stood up, I could feel the pressure weighing down on my leg. I just took a deep breath. Therapy started, and as I began to walk, I began singing the song the youth from the youth ministry Queens, that was birthed out by my daughter, with every step I take: "Every step I make, I make in you Jesus. Every move I make, I move in you Jesus!!!" Yes, my mind went back to those Queens meeting with them on Saturdays. They were truly a blessing. I began to feel like I was getting stronger as I walked. Therapy was good that day. I really do believe that it was the best therapy session I had since I had come home with little pain. I was able to breathe and walk without walker.

After the therapy was over, we sat down to check my blood pressure. The nurse wanted to listen to my heart and said, "Mrs. Nathaniel, I think I need to call your doctor." I asked, "Why?" He said, "Because I don't like the way your heart sounds; it's beating too fast." My INR had gone up to a 3.5, meaning that my blood was getting too thin. I looked at my brother Rickey, then at the nurse, and said, "You can call her; however, I'm not going back to the hospital!! The nurse was given the approval to sit with me for a little while longer to monitor me. He checked the INR again and called my doctor with the update. She said, "I want you to go into the ER." I said, "No, I'm not going to go to the ER. I'm tired of going back and forth to the hospital."

I remember that day after the nurse left, my brother left to pick my daughter up from school. She had continued her classes at a nearby small college. My daughter walked in, and she was carrying at the time. I thought it was just my grand baby, but we eventually found out that she was carrying twins. And when she walked in, I remember saying in my mind, *Lord Jesus, let me live, so I can see my grandchild.* I begin to believe God for every promise that He said and one of the promises I held on to was when He said with long life that He would satisfy me. I begin to say that every day with long life Lord you're going to satisfy me, and I don't just want to see my grandchild but I'm going to see my grandchild and live and I'm going to see him or her grow up. Later we found out my daughter was carrying twins, so they gave me double the reason to live. I strongly put my faith in the Lord.

I knew my daughter was going to need me. She was going to need my strength. She's carrying two babies. Lord, I need strength. I need strength while she's carrying. If she can see that I'm strong, then she could be strong too. I began to get strength, and by my birthday in September, I was standing up strongly, getting myself ready to receive my two grandchildren. Hence, I tell you, I believed without question!!! I believed when he breathed through my nostrils in the dream. He was breathing new breath in me. He was giving me a new life.

My nurse was instructed to have me check my INR later that night after having dinner. I remember the dream when the hands fed me a green substance. I shared it with my husband when he came home and asked him to make me some spinach. Hallelujah, the next morning when the nurse came, my INR was 2.7!!! Eventually my doctor put the order in for the INR machine, which was truly a blessing to have!! I was able to monitor my blood more closely.

They said that my leg would never be normal again. I would walk with a limp, and I would probably need to walk with a cane. That my leg would always carry fluid in it, which would always have weight to it. I dragged my left leg for about three months. In November, I was able to stand up on Thanksgiving to enjoy with my family.

During the time of the blood clot, my prayer was for the Body of Christ to continue in serving the Lord and to remain steadfast in their faith. I shared my concerns with the Lord as a leader. One thing I kept in mind was that we were a body of believers, whom the Lord was healing, delivering, saving, and setting free. Families were coming in being healed and restored. Of course, the devil would attempt to bother my mind regarding my pastoral care duties as well as just not being able to fully recover. As I reclined back on my living room sofa, the Holy Spirit began to minister to me. I remember Him comforting me so clearly as I heard in my spirit, "Don't try to identify where you're at, it's not about the place where you're at now. The question is, 'Do you believe while you're in this place? Don't try to understand it; don't try to identify what's happening, just believe.

In December, we began to prepare for the arrival of my twin granddaughters. The Lord gave me a double anointing to cause me to live. I call them my strawberries, because strawberries are good for the heart, and truly, they were good for my heart. You might be going through a time of your life where you may be looking to man, a friend, a coworker, or somebody to get you out or bring you through. I encourage you to believe every word God has spoken about you! Oh! I sing the song "There is power in the blood" with such great appreciation!!! Glory to the Father for His precious Son Jesus and His blood intertwining with my blood!!!! *Christ's blood intertwined with my blood*, therefore, if anyone is in Christ, he is a new creation. Old things have passed away, behold, all things have become new. I was pleading for the blood of Jesus for my total healing. The power of the blood of the Lamb healed me!! By His stripes, every sickness and disease has been destroyed in my life in Jesus Christs' precious name Amen! Oftentimes, we don't believe when the scripture tells us that by His stripes we are healed. I tell you today BELIEVE!!!

# CHAPTER 8

# Made Whole

In March 2006, I heard about a conference that burned in my soul for about two to three weeks. I kept hearing the voice of God saying, "Come, come, come, come," and every time I heard the voice, it got stronger and stronger. I began to yearn deeply more and more. I shared the event with a few sisters in Christ at the time. They were beyond excited about going!! We decided that we would take a flight to Atlanta where the conference was being held. For most of us, if not all of us, it was our first ever flight. On our way to the airport the snow started coming down heavy I said Wow!!! In the beginning of April look at this snow!! My stomach began to shake, because this was my first flight. My mind began to wander, but then I kept hearing, "Come," and as we got closer to the airport, I began to feel a calmness come over me. While sitting in the airport, laughing and talking with the other sisters, all I could think about was going up beyond the clouds. All I could think about was going to another place or a place in which I've never been before. I heard the voice again, "Come."

As we boarded the plane and going to our seats, I remembered the green bags I had purchased to give to each one of the sisters. In my green bag, I had my Bible. I had the Word of God. I had the shield. I had my armor. All I was thinking was that as soon as I get in my seat, I was going to take out my Bible and start reading. Because it was my first flight, I did not know protocol that once you were aboard, the flight attendants would be sharing some safety measures. My bag had to be kept away until we were in the air. I couldn't wait to get my Bible in my hand and start reading it.

As we took off to head to Atlanta, I remember pulling my green bag from under the seat that was in front of me, pulling out my Bible, and just looking out of the window at the clouds—thinking that it had to be God who was calling me to this place, because had I never imagined that I would fly. I opened my Bible; honestly, I can't remember the chapter, but I know that I had opened it. I don't remember where I was reading. I remember that I was looking out of the window, just being above the clouds and knowing that we were in the second heavens.

Understanding the pilot was flying the plane however we were in the Lord's hands. I chuckled at this moment, because I remember that as we were on the plane, a few sisters who had never flown before began to cry and sing. All I could say was, "We're on a mission headed to Atlanta Georgia." So much was going through my heart, mind, and stomach! I believe my stomach was wobbly because of the excitement. We arrived at the hotel to see a place that I'd never seen before. I was truly excited about being able to get into a place that I knew the voice of God was calling me to.

There were many sacrifices made to get to Atlanta. Oh my, the stay!! There were six of us, and we went into one hotel room that had one bed. We were in a tight space, but I'm often reminded that sometimes you would have to be in a tight, uncomfortable place—just for a moment. Sometimes in those uncomfortable places, the Lord would speak to us, if we would just listen.

In the first night of the conference, we were told to wear all white. Upon our arrival at the Georgia Dome, I felt the Holy Spirit upon seeing all the white. His presence was all around us. We had VIP seats. We were two rows away from the stage. As I got closer to where we were to sit, the Holy Spirit began to redirect me. I perceived in my spirit, "Although you were reserved to sit in the front, this is not where I want you to sit." Upon hearing this, I looked at my other sisters to say, "I know VIP seats are reserved for us, but this is not where we were supposed to be sitting." As we made our way, they looked at me with surprise, as if questioning, "What are you saying?" I said, "I'm saying, we can't sit here; we have to go where the Holy Spirit is directing us." He began to lead us to the upper level of the Georgia Dome on the right-hand side of us and to the left-hand side of those who were going to be speaking. We made our way up, moving quickly through the crowds of people. People looked at us as if we were kind of out of our minds, because we had VIP badges. The reason why we had to go up to the second level was that when God begins to order your foot-steps, you should obey, being in a place of knowing that God will do something great. We made our way to the place where the Lord ordered our footsteps to sit. That space happened to be our space for the entire duration of the conference.

On our third night in the conference, one of the preachers, who was minis-tering that night, was a preacher whom I had a dream about a little while after graduating from high school. I didn't know who he was in my dream. I saw him and heard his voice, but I didn't know who he was. In my mind, I began to go back and think about that dream. As I saw this preacher take the stage and being introduced, I began to reflect. Suddenly something clicked in my spirit, something hit my soul, and I began to think about how my mother's friend was cleaning out her library and she sent me home these tapes along with VCR tapes and books of this anointed vessel of God known around the world. It begins to line up.

I began to think about the dream I had of this honorable man of God. As I thought about the books that were given to me, I looked at this man repeatedly. After watching him on TV until now, when I saw him in the same room where I was, I began to give glory honor, and praise to the Lord! Why? Because through the voice of God, I heard it loud and clear that this is why we had to move from our VIP seats. The Lord was going to speak directly to us. As the service went on, the Holy Spirit poured out upon us during worship. This preacher stood tall, and his voice filled the Georgia Dome.

He begins to minister. I honestly do not remember the scripture where he came from, because all I could take from that night was what he mentioned when he looked over to the left of him, which was to our right. He looked up, pointed in our direction, and said, "It's six of you right over here in this section; you sacrificed to get here. In fact, some of you are sleeping in one hotel room, where some of you are sleeping on the bed and some on the floor." We all knew that he was speaking directly to us. The Holy Spirit was speaking through him. A fire fell on me, and I began to bless God for the man of God, because I know that God was using him that night, and that's all that' was stuck in me. He said, "You will leave this conference and go back to your city, and you will cause a great impact in it." I was blank for the rest of the evening.

I remember going to the last two days of the conference, already empowered from the word that was released over us. I remember that as we boarded the plane to come back to Philadelphia, we couldn't do anything but laugh and cry at our time and just know that God had spoken to us individually!!!

As we landed back in Philadelphia and went to retrieve our luggage, I began to see the women. There were plenty of men in the midst of us, but the women were struggling, grabbing their luggage from the carousel. Many of them were carrying so much on their shoulders. The Holy Spirit had me stand there, and it felt like I was a merry go round. I got dizzy, and I remember the Holy Spirit say, "Do you see that my daughters are carrying so much luggage? They carry so much weight, they're burdened down, they're heavy, they're broken, there's no one there to help them with their luggage."

I remember that after we got back home, the days and weeks went by, and then on one day in May 2006, I was lying in my bed praying for my mother. The Holy Spirit told me to wrap myself in my prayer shawl. As I did so, the Holy Spirit started speaking the word "whole" I wrote the word down and said, "Father, what are you saying?" He took me back to when we were in the Philadelphia International Airport. He said, "Women are helping other lives to excel!!! Wilt thou be made whole?" I began to bless God and thank him. I remember writing this out on my yellow tablet in my bedroom, and that night, the *WHOLE* ministry was born.

Our faith tells us that all things are possible with God, so whatever you may have been going through, whatever you may have experienced in life, no matter what heartbreak, abandonment, disappointments, the scripture tells us that Jesus asks a woman a question, "Wilt thou be made whole?" She looked at the Lord, and the Bible says that in that same hour she was made whole.

We often think in our lives that it takes another human being, money, prosperity, or even perhaps love from another person to make us whole. It takes elevation or opportunity for us to come from a place of brokenness and be made whole. However, we must know that Jesus came to give us life, and that not only did he come to give us life but also that we may have it more abundantly. We can live an abundant life!!! The obstacles in living an abundant life are living in the past living, living in a place of pain, and living in a place of unforgiveness, bitterness, frustration, aggravation, sickness, and disease. But to be made whole is to allow the Lord to heal every area of your life. You can't deal with it from the surface, but you must get to the root of it. That means sometimes you may have to revisit way back in your childhood and forgive the person or people who hurt you. Believe it or not, this is why so many people remain broken. They don't allow themselves to deal with the pain of the past … think about that for a moment, pain of the past!! That's it the past!!! Let it go and know that once you have accepted your Lord and Savior Jesus Christ, he will lead you, guide you, and direct you into all truth. When you put your hand in His hand, it means that you are saying that you trust Him with your life.

Think about it, God has created your life, and He knows everything about you. He knows your beginning, middle, and your ending. He knows what you're in—your failures, setbacks, abandonment, and comebacks. He knows all your heartache and pain. He knows the place that you're in even right now. You may be in a place where you might feel like there is no coming out. It may be dark. It may be a place where there's a lot of pain. But to be made whole is when you know that Jesus will come into your life, and he will bring light to heal you of your pain. For each of you, there is a cut that has salt in it, so that every time you touch it or think about it, it brings about pain, hurt, frustration, and devastation—all of which brings about destruction. When you allow Jesus to come in, He will place His anointing on that cut. To be made whole, is when you know that Jesus has touched the wounds, and when he puts his anointing on it, nothing else can cause pain in that wound again

One of the most amazing things that came out of the *Whole Ministry* was a gathering of the Lord's daughters by the water!!! I often say by the sea is where you will find me. Jesus was often found by the sea. On the sea is where he would perform many miracles. He specialized in storms. There would be times when he would call his disciples out on the shore, and they would find themselves in the storm. One night, there were some fishermen fishing all night, but they couldn't catch anything. Jesus showed up and told them to cast down their nets on the other side. And when they brought up their nets and did so, there were a multitude of fish.

In 2006, the Holy Spirit told me to take his daughters to the water. I didn't understand it. At first, I saw a lot of women standing in all white along the seashore with their hands lifted. I began to speak to the Lord and asked him what He was showing me, and he showed me his daughters at the water—worshiping him, praising him, and giving him all glory and honor. I spoke to my sisters and shared with them what I saw in the vision. I told them the Lord Instructed me to take his daughters to the water. Women Worshiping at the Water was birthed out in the year 2006. I thought it was just the six of us who journeyed down to Atlanta for the conference April of that year.

As I began to seek the Lord about it, I began to see more and more women and made mention about it to a few other sisters outside of our church. And before I knew it, six women turned into forty-nine women. The Holy Spirit instructed me to go down into Wildwood Crest, New Jersey, and as I went, He would instruct me about what to do and I obeyed all I heard.

In September 2006, the Lord gave me the colors for the women to wear and what the colors meant. His daughters were to come to the water and allow that time to be an intimate time between them and their Lord and Savior Jesus Christ. The Lord desires for his daughters to come to him and worship him. This was going to be a season when they will come and bow down in his presence and he will perform miracles in their lives; deliverance and healing was going to take place. We were going to see signs and miracles. Everything was happening very fast before my eyes as I had begun to move out and do what the Holy Spirit was instructing me to do. It became clear, and I saw that we would need a bus to take the women down to the shore. As I began to register the women, I remember feeling overwhelmed. The bus began to fill up...

The Holy Spirit started showing me what to do. One of the things He showed me was that there were going to be baptisms. I paused at that and said, "Lord, baptisms?" While I was thinking that he was going to say, "They were to be done in the pool of the hotel," He showed me out in the middle of the ocean. Now I understood the dream that I had some years prior with me riding on a white horse with wings in the middle of the ocean. I always felt this dream had a spiritual meaning to it. I said to the Holy Spirit, "Really me? And the middle of the sea? I can't swim." And the Lord said yes to baptisms and dedications for purification and salvation.

Taking a deep breath, I remember making the announcement during our meet and greet, asking, "Who of you have already been baptized and who desire to be baptized?" Many began to ask questions about baptism. Some had been baptized as children but desired to be baptized as adults. The Lord was confirming what I saw and heard in the vision.

Our very first time going the Holy spirit moved mighty. We followed His instructions and were excited about the worship experience. We had to get up between the hours of 4 a.m. and 5 a.m. to prepare ourselves for 6 a.m. worship. We were down by the sea before the sunrise to meet our Lord and Savior Jesus Christ during an intimate time of worship. The Lord dealt with his daughters individually. The Holy Spirit showed up strongly in the midst of us. Tears were flowing; hands were lifted; and the waves were rushing in like a mighty rushing wind. The fellowship was awesome sisters were sharing their testimonies and their struggles. We witnessed lives transformed that weekend!! We departed to come back to Philadelphia. I received a call from the hotel manager with great excitement in her voice. She said, "I don't know all you were doing down there by the ocean, but it caused a whale to wash up on the shore." I said, "No way!" I told her we were worshiping and praising the Lord. She said, "Watch the news later this evening. The exact spot where you all were worshiping is where the whale came." I said, "See, they always pick with me and say I'm seeing things." I told them that morning that I saw something out there!!! Lives were being changed all around us. As they continue to be changed even until today, many women have journeyed along with us over the years. The spirit of the Lord has always fallen upon us at the designated spot.

One year during our 6 a.m. worship, the fog was very heavy as we began to head down. It literally appeared as if the first Heavens had come down and kissed our foreheads. His presence was so heavy that his daughters began to fall at his feet. Some were so caught up that they did not even realize that they were so far out in the ocean!!! Many daughters came with a lot of unforgiveness and desired to be healed of different elements in their bodies. The word of the Lord came to me and said, "Forgive, and set yourself free." The unforgiveness in their hearts was allowing them to carry bitterness and pain, which was causing boils and cysts to appear in different parts of their body. We saw instant healing. Hallelujah, daughters were coming to the water, getting what the Holy Spirit was desiring them to have. He ushered them into an authentic place of worship.

The scripture tells us that those who worship the Lord must worship Him in spirit and in truth. I remember during an evening worship, one year the Holy Spirit fell upon us, and healing and deliverance happened right there at the water's edge. Over the last fifteen years, we've seen mother-and-daughter relationships healed; sisters', nieces', and cousins' relationships restored. We have seen daughters identify their identity, mothers and wives becoming who they were destined to be. Every year, the Holy Spirit has visited us in a very special way. The people vacationing in the nearby hotels are always impacted by our presence.

One year, a local cab company called us "the women in purple" during the season of praying and seeking the Lord for 2020 Gathering. The Holy Spirit kept saying, "I'm going to make the difference." I honestly didn't think too hard on it. I just praised Him for whatever he was going to do. Our theme that year was fifty daughters to the water in 2020. During our 6 a.m. worship, the beach turned golden from sunrise that morning. As we worshiped, the rain began to fall gently upon us, and my Lord the Holy Spirit fell! I remember the sound of his daughters praising him and shouting that "There's a double rainbow" as I turned and saw the double rainbow!!! I remember taking off, running toward it, and honestly felt like I ran through it after we left worship. In my spirit, I heard the Holy Spirit say, "Remember the promises I made unto you!!"

On Sunday morning during the 6 a.m. worship and baptism, we saw something we had never seen happen before. As we turned, we witnessed the Holy Spirit usher people from their balconies as well as those who were walking the beach. They came and stood around us. There were believers and nonbelievers. The waves were crashing in!!! Oh my! The waves were very heavy. The Lord was blessing his people. Some people asked for prayer, and some wanted to know what was happening out in the ocean. It was truly an amazing time. I had the privilege of meeting and speaking with a priest from out of the country. The Holy Spirit blessed him right where he was standing. He said, "He had never seen baptism being done out in the ocean before."

Since the Lord had called us to the water, I came in touch with a part of me I no longer saw—the beach as a vacation spot. Yes, while still enjoying my husband, children, grandchildren, and family, I'm always sensitive to the spirit. And if He calls me by the sea, I don't think twice about breaking away. During the season of preparation for annual gathering, the Holy Spirit often calls me several times by the sea. I must inform my husband when the Lord is calling me. Sometimes he would join me, but other times, I would pack my bag, get in my car, and travel down by the sea. There's not been a time when the Holy Spirit didn't show up.

One time, after praying and worship, I just began to take pictures of the waves and the birds. As I played my worship music the little birds were drawn to the sound. I never looked at the pictures until about 4 a.m. the next morning, and the Holy Spirit told me to look back at the day. He was showing me what He' had suddenly called me to the see. When I started looking through my phone at the pictures, I almost lost my breath. My name appeared to be written in the sand. I sent the pictures both to my son and my daughter after 4 a.m. but didn't get a response from them until later that morning. They both saw what I saw. I shared it with our church, and I asked them what they saw in the picture. Some saw my name, whereas some had to take a second look. This was during a very critical time in my life. The enemy attacked everything attached to me; the Holy Spirit snatched me from the hands of the enemies and ushered me into his presence. He called me by my name!!!

Another time I was called down to a section of the island that I had never been to in all my twenty-seven years of visiting.

While out on the pier, looking out, I was recording and taking pictures in my phone. This time while recording, the Holy Spirit turned me around again and again, and He blew my mind, an image appeared as the Son of God walking in the sky. I could hear in my spirit lo I'm with you." All I could do was give Him glory!! When in the presence of the Lord, if you're broken you will instantly be made WHOLE!!!

When we think of the word "whole," we think of entire, complete, full, perfect, intact, total, and unbroken. Oftentimes, we believe that we are so far in a broken place that none of these things could happen to us, or nothing can make us whole. We think that we cannot overcome. The things that have happened to us in life could cause us to remain in a place of brokenness. Sometimes we think that whatever has happened in our childhood, young adult life, or even in old age, we cannot be in a place of being made whole.

Life tends to bring to us storms, situations, chaos, confusion, heartbreak, setback, disappointment, childhood issues, molestation, divorce, sickness, disease of addiction, trauma, self-destruction, bitterness, and verbal, emotional, and sometimes physical abuse. These things happen in life, and they cause us to be broken. However, none of these things are too hard for the Lord to heal. He specializes in healing. His anointing destroys these things that become yokes in our lives. His desire is for you to be healed and whole, so you can walk in total victory!

# CHAPTER 9

# Walking Into Destiny With The Devil

In my walk, I often think about the many battles and the things that came to try to hinder my progress. Whether they were work-related, business-related, family-related, or physical-health-related situations, I decided I was going to hold on to the Word of God.

In your life, you must know that you have the keys that you need to lead you into destiny, and that you have been called with a purpose. You must also remember who you are and who you belong to. My personal relationship with my Lord and Savior Jesus Christ means everything to me. When trials and tribulations come, when sickness and disease come, and when LIFE happens, I constantly remind myself that the Lord is with me. He promised us that He would neither leave us nor forsake us!!! Oh, how I love when He reminds me, "I'm with you always, even unto the end of the world." I hear these words deep in my heart, especially when I'm in a battle!! There are so many things that we battle in this world.

You must yield your spirit and stand still to know which battles belong to you and which ones belong to our Lord Jesus Christ. I began to see a lot of things coming against me. I had to learn very early that if I was going to walk in my destiny, then I had to remember that we wrestle not against flesh and blood!!! We have an enemy, and he has his demons who try to fight us!!! Who try to stop and block us!!!! When I learned that I was given all the power to overcome and defeat the enemy, I kept my mind on all that was given to me. What was given to me? The promises from God.

Whatever time of the season, if there was opposition, I knew that I had to keep going. Sometimes it wasn't easy, and then sometimes, it was like a breeze. I think about a period in life when I was having a very hard time in my business. I was feeling like I was standing on top of a cliff, ready to throw in everything. There were many things that were coming up against the business. I knew I had to keep my mind and heart on Jesus. He did promise us that He would keep those in a perfect peace whose mind stayed on Him. The storms were raging all at once, and I didn't have any physical strength. I became numb. I believe the Lord allowed the numbness so that I wouldn't feel the beating of the waves. At one point, it really got scary. Have you ever been in a place where you couldn't see anything?!! I mean eyes wide open, but just pure darkness!

I remember sitting in my office at my desk, while it was raining. I was looking out of the window; the Holy Spirit brought my attention to my plants along the wall. They had dried out because I was not watering them. I would come into the office, be overwhelmed by everything, and forget to water them. I heard deep in my spirit, "These plants have stood the test that although they have lost their color, they have not lost their firmness. Now stand up and water them. And just as you water them, I'm pouring out upon you!!" I got up from my desk and began to water them not only with water but also with my tears!! I felt a strength come upon me!! I began to give the Lord all the glory and honor. Before the week was over, I saw the leaves turning back green!!! He made me lie down in green pastures!!! I was surely being restored!! God gave me the business, and because he gave it to me, it was a part of my destiny. I had to hold on to it.

You must remember in life when God gives you something for you to get from one place to the next. You can't give up on it!!! You must hold on to it and keep fighting for it!! I tell my clients all the time, "This too shall pass; trouble doesn't last always; it doesn't come to stay, it's a restoration day!!! Don't give up!!! Don't ever forget that what God releases to you in your life is for a purpose." I had to hold on to the business because I knew He said that it will not only be for restoration of license but also for the restoration of souls. He gave me a platform to spread the Gospel of Jesus Christ.

When people were coming in whatever state, I was able to share about Jesus with them. I was able to encourage them. The Holy Spirit would begin to fill the room. They were ushered into a place where they weren't before they walked in the door. I knew that having the business was a part of my destiny. It was going to take me from one place to the next. When opposition came, the battles came in the business. There were times when I had to spiritually fight. I didn't realize I was fighting. I had to go in with my eyes closed. I couldn't look at what I saw, but I had to keep believing in what I heard.

What was it that I heard? You started this with $4 and faith!!! Neither business loans nor government or city assistance!!! I knew my faith would take me through anything that I was facing. I kept at it; I kept pushing and pushing!!! I went from one location to the next, and then, to the next!!! Each location had its own purpose!!! Hallelujah, thank you Jesus, another battle with the devil while walking in my destiny was having to get to the place of knowing that no matter what hurt I went through, the Lord will heal me.

I came to a time in the ministry when I had to pause for several months, because I didn't understand what was going on. My only mission was to share the Gospel of Jesus, lead people to Him, share His love, His compassion, His healing, and His deliverance, which would eventually lead them to salvation. I met so many people from so many different lifestyles and situations. I poured my heart, my time, my resources, and sometimes money out to them. I remember that during these months, I would converse with the Lord. How and why was I always put in a position to nurture people and eventually turn around in the end to be hurt by those same people? I had to remember that it was a part of my destiny. Experiencing the hurt and pain from people, because that's the spirit that they were often needed to be delivered from. I did not appreciate the fact that I was made available to them and once they received what they had to, the enemy would send to them something to get distracted.

I humbly received many whom the Lord was calling, and on the very same platform, those very same people found an opportunity to come against me and turn on me literally!!! All I wanted to see was them walking toward their destiny. They would try to speak with me privately but would deny to acknowledging that they knew me publicly. But that too was a spirit the Lord allowed me to see very early. I allowed some of it to go by me, but I had to address some of it. Even people who were very close to me and had known me all my life they would take a knife and jab me in my back or chest, while all I tried to do was help them get in a better position!! They tried to spit in my face, talked about me, lied to me, and accused me of whatever they could find to bring me pain.

It's chilling to know that some of them were being used by the Lord to shape me into who I am today. Wow!! I just had a moment … they had to walk that walk with me because it was a part of my destiny … it became a part of my life is faith … The Holy Spirit would remind me not to look at their faces!!! I understood that I was still being blessed in the midst of it, because although they were a part of my destiny, I came to know that I was a part of theirs, and that was one of the greatest breakthroughs that I ever received. Knowing that I was a part of someone's deliverance was simply unexplainable. It was a deep-breath moment, because through it, all you can say is, "Lord, I pray that I have been pleasing in your sight." This is when I knew that I became that yielded vessel.

When you have become a yielded vessel, are walking into your destiny, and the devil is present, remember your yes!!! Your yes begins to speak to you and reminds you about when you said yes to the Lord. You have yielded your very being to Him. No matter what comes your way or what the enemy brings in your journey, you know that in the end you have the victory. Knowing that you have said yes to the Lord will bring you to a place of just questioning, "Am I hearing right? Or am I seeing right?" Being that yielded vessel means that you have given up your mind, body, spirit, and soul!!! You have allowed Him to be Lord in your Life.

There are things that are toxic, and you can't allow them to stay in your mind, because having a toxic mindset will distract you from your destiny. Being distracted will prevent you from following directions and instructions given to you from the Lord. Directions lead you into destiny. Distractions come in many ways. I've witnessed distractions coming through people. I'm instantly reminded that it's not the person but the spirit that's in them. The enemy uses that spirit to distract you. It can be operating in people that are very close to you. Someone you wouldn't even imagine. I used to hear the older saints say the devil will use the closest thing to you!! Well, I thought about that thing!!!! The thing could be something materialistic or a person!!

I've watched the devil use many people that were close to me. In the midst of them being used, I always kept that in my mind and stayed focused on Jesus while pursuing my destiny. Destiny is just not here on earth. Destiny is around the throne of God. That's where I'm destined to be. Coming into the knowledge of knowing this, I wouldn't allow anything or anyone to stop me. When people hear the word "destiny," they think about goals and dreams. They think about places that you would reach after going through a process of doing something. When I think about destiny, I think about that eternal place that's true destiny. That's where we are all destined to go.

Think about the time when you were traveling on an airplane, you would either have a straight flight or a layover flight, one way or round trip. The flight attendant would make the announcement saying, "You can get your luggage at your final destination." When I think about that, I set my mind on my destination, which is not here. I just have a layover here. The enemy will walk with you throughout life on your journey, and he will throw in some stones or some glass to cut you—sickness, disease, manipulation, all kinds of things. These will be the distractions. Once I understood distractions and why they came, I had the power to even dictate them!! I wouldn't allow the distractions to operate in my life. No matter how many came, I always knew in my heart that I would overcome them.

You need to know today you have the victory. You may be walking or running right now, and there's a distraction that's right alongside you. Know today that you have the power, and it can't stop your destiny. I like to call it *destiny's distractions!!* Whatever distraction that's there in your life right now, remember that you have the control. We have been given power and authority in this life that we live in. You have the authority to control what's going to be in your life. If you allow the devil to bring distractions to stop you from reaching your destiny, then you will be the one who will be sitting and questioning. I'm reminded this verse through the scriptures: You did run well but who hindered you? Do you know hindrance is a distraction?

I think about how God knows all things. He allows distractions to come, however, the greatest side of this is that we know the distractions are coming from the enemy to stop or block us. We must know if God is allowing a certain thing to happen. He uses it for His glory. Take a deep breath and hold on to it!! There were several moments in my life that the Holy Spirit would speak softly, "It's for my glory." I remember one night in our shut in. all night prayer; I was going through some battles. While lying at the altar, all I could hear was, "It's for my glory." I began to weep and tell the Lord thanks! Out of my mouth came, "Yes, it is for your glory!!"

God allows us to go through things in life so that He will get the glory. No man will be able to have His glory. He doesn't even desire to share His glory. He said in His Word that He wouldn't share His glory with any man. I began to say, "Yes, Lord." When it got deep in my spirit, heart, and soul, I knew that whatever the outcome was going to be, it would be for my good! Your trials and tribulations come to make you stronger. While you're in it, He will step in and begin to move things. He will begin to shift things around in your life so that you can see Him. Sometimes if we get it easy, we forget all about God's heart and focus on His hand.

The word of the Lord came to Jeremiah, and he said, "Before I formed thee in the belly, I knew you, and before thou came forth out of the womb, I sanctified you and ordained you a prophet to the nation."

Walking into your destiny with the devil is very important for you to know your identity. While walking this journey into my destiny one of the scriptures I hold on to also in Jeremiah for I know the thoughts that I think toward you saith the Lord thoughts of peace and not of evil to give you an expected end.

# CHAPTER 10

## Restoration

In 1992, I remember sitting in my room at my parents' home. I had been home for a year out of work by choice. I decided to stay home and help my sister with her baby girl while she attends and finishes school. While sitting in my room, I thought, *Now is the time for me to start getting up and getting out.* I remember going into prayer during this time. My prayer life wasn't as intense as it is now. I knew that my faith told me that I can talk to God, and He would respond.

I remember saying to God that I wanted to go out and get a job. I began looking through the *Daily News*, asking different people about employment. I was led by something now I know was the Holy Spirit—to go back through the youth program that I had once gone through as a teenager for summer employment. I remember going to the office. The name of the organization was the Urban Coalition at the time. I remember seeing this woman who was very sweet and small in stature. She called me into her office after reviewing my application. When I sat at her desk, she said, "How soon are you ready to work?" I replied, "I'm ready to work today!!!" She said, "really, you're ready to work today?" I said, "Yes ma'am." She said, "Okay, go out in the lobby and have a seat; I'm going to make a few calls." I remember this day as if it was just last week. I set out in the waiting area for about I believe maybe about an hour until she called me back into her office. She said, "I think I may have something for you." I looked at her, smiling, and said, "Really?" She said, "Yes. Will you be able to go to Spring Garden Street now? Do you know where it is?" I said, "No, but if you tell me, I can find it." We were at Broad and Arch at the time. She said, "You can get on the 'C' bus and go down to Broad and Spring Garden, get off, and get the 43 number bus, and it will take you to 923 Spring Garden Street. There's a gentleman there by the name Mr. H, and he's waiting now to see you. I said thank you so much.

Walking out of the office, getting on the elevator, going down, and going out as soon as I went out there was a "C" bus right there. I jumped on and got down to Broad and Spring Garden. I didn't see the 43 number bus, so I decided to walk from Broad and Spring Garden to 9th and Spring Garden. I remember walking into this small office with a glass partition. A young man by the name of Mr. S greeted me. He asked, "How can I help you?" I said, "I'm here to see Mr. H." He said, "Have a seat." I was called into his office where he interviewed me. I honestly can't remember all the questions; however, I will never forget him saying, "If you were hired, how soon could you start?" Just as I had told to Mrs. T, I said, "I can start today!!!"

I remember him taking his pen and putting it on his chin. He said, "Okay, great! Nice meeting you, Maryann. You'll hear from me in a few days with my decision." That was on a Tuesday, April 21, 1992. Mr. H called me on Friday and said, "Will you be able to start on Monday, the 27th? I said, "Yes sir!!!" This was a major time in my life that I had no idea of what was getting ready to take place!!!! Instantly I embraced something far more than I imagined. My Life began to change, and I didn't know how great of a change it was. I started working at this little office that was very powerful and impactful. It was small yet huge. I'm reminded when the scripture asks a question: Could any good thing come out of Nazareth? It was a business for driver license restoration. Wow! The business was in operation for restoring people's driving privileges. I worked there in that establishment for seven years. I was hired as a receptionist, then got promoted to a secretary, and then to office manager. Later in the years I was blessed to be able to bring my two sisters alongside me. Wow! We had quite the favor upon our lives, and we didn't even realize it then. My sister next to me, Claresa, and my baby sister, Carrie, was in junior high school. The Lord was preparing us for something we didn't have a clue of. Something amazing happened while working with Mr. H in that little office!! I had the privilege of meeting some amazing people!!!

I was the one answering the phones most of the time. Sometimes I would close my eyes, answering and wishing I could close my ears!! There was this gentleman who would always call about his case. This one day, he called with an attitude. He always would sound so upset. I had got fed up with his calls and said, "Sir, you paid your money. You need to come and see who you paid your money to." He decided to come to the office that day. My coworker and I were rotating in greeting clients as they came in. I didn't know then what I know now: It was God who allowed me to say to my coworker, "I'll attend to him." I did not even know who he was!!! He walked in and stood at the counter. Something hit my stomach and my life changed forever. He came in as my client and instantly in the Heaven, he left as my husband. Not on the same day as my husband, but spiritually it was sealed in the heavens. As he walked up to the counter, I said, "You must be Greg Nathaniel." He said, "You must be MaryAnn!!" And from that point, it was nothing but smiles. I told him to have a seat and I'll let Mr. H know he was here. I didn't have to pull his file because it was already on Mr. D's desk. He sat out in the waiting area for about ten to fifteen minutes. I was then instructed to bring him back to Mr. H's office.

Mr. D's office was directly in front of my desk. All I could hear was Mr. Nathaniel trying to get my attention. I turned and looked in the office, and he asked, "Can I take you for dinner?" I just looked and smiled. Eventually, his meeting was over, and as he walked by my stomach fluttered. He called the office the next day, telling me to take his number and give him a call.

I waited for several weeks to call. When I called, his mother answered the phone, and the first question she asked me was, "Are you saved?" I almost hung the phone up. I told her, "I believe in Jesus, but I think I'm in a backslidden condition." She said, "Well you need to get saved sweetheart. Gregory is not

**83**

here; I'll let him know that you called." A few days later, I called again, and we finally started talking. We've been talking ever since. He said when he laid eyes on me, he had said to himself, "Mm G, you can make something like her your wife!!!"

I eventually had to take over his case. They had given up on him, and I had an interest in him, so because I had an interest in him, I had an interest in his case. I started looking at his case closely. I began to do some strategizing and before I knew it. His driving privileges were restored. He went from being a client to being an associate, then we started dating. He became my friend then my boyfriend on to being my fiancé, and from being my fiancé to being my husband!!!! I fell in love with one of my clients, who is now my husband—my GREGORY!! And this is where it all began to click!!!

I began to embrace it after marrying my husband and having our daughter. I began to hear the voice even more when I was young and married at the age of twenty-two. I never doubted our union; I just wanted to be sure I would be the wife to the man I said "I do" to. I wanted to be the wife God called me to be.

You might wonder what this has to do with restoration, because it was something missing in both of us. He didn't have his driver license; it needed to be restored, and the Lord used the messy situation to be turned into a message of restoration and love. We were blessed with our miracle baby girl Claresa (Boop) the same year we were married in 1994!!! And the Lord surprised us and blessed us with our Son Gregory Jr. (DAAD) in 1996!!!! I worked with the firm for a few more years until 1998, then my season there was up.

I remember we had a situation in the office that led me to walk out, and when I walked out, it led to an argument. I made the decision that I wasn't going back!!!! Finally, I was told that I was being fired for insubordination. I wasn't upset at all. My thought was, *I will be able to be home with my children.* At least I thought I would.... I was home for several months.

One night I was sitting in my living room my husband had recently purchased me a computer. I got up and went over to the computer desk. As I got on the computer, I had a vision. I put in the computer what I saw. I remember that night shutting it down and thinking to myself, *no, that can't be*. About a week or so later, I received a phone call from an attorney by the name of Mr. C, asking me to assist him with some license restoration work, and I began to talk to him about me being home. He asked me to meet him down at the court so we could go over the case. He really didn't have an interest in the restoration part. I was back in the business of doing license restoration work.

The vision that I had previously was that of MaryAnn's License Express, then I thought about my sisters, Claresa & Carrie. I talked to Claresa about us getting started in our own license restoration business.

On March 11, 1999, M&C License Express was born. I started the business out of my home with $4 and faith. Almost every day my husband would leave money on the table for our daughter. This day he left $5 dollars. I remember taking her to our neighborhood store she wanted chips and juice, I saw the pies were two for a dollar my grandfather David favorites. I was getting ready to buy two however instantly I changed my mind. I paid for her snack and returned home. I had to order paperwork from the messenger for the case counsel had call me about. When I called to make the request the agent at the messenger's office said it's normally ten dollars but for you Maryann it's $4. She knew me from working at the restoration place where I was previously employed. I tell the world Faith, four dollars and my black-and-white composition book led me on a journey!! I started working from my living room. One day, I had to go down to the court to pick up some paperwork on Spring Garden Street. My mother would drive with me, because I would have my babies in the back of the car. My mother noticed the building as we turned on 11th Street. It had a "for rent sign" on it. She said you should get the number! I pulled over and got the phone number. By faith I called the number and scheduled an appointment to take a tour of the building.

When we started the business from my home, we didn't have much advertisement. Financially I wasn't prepared to give what the landlord was asking for. We left from seeing the property, but my husband told him that we would get back to him. In my mind, while walking through the property it was by

FAITH that M&C License Express had already occupied the space. When we arrived home, my husband said, "Are you ready for this? Is this what you want to do?" I said, "Yes." He said, "Call the landlord tomorrow and tell him that we will see him on Friday!!!"

Hallelujah, we moved in October 1999 and remained there till April 2006, being there for seven years. I remember the Holy Spirit saying, "This will not only be for the restoration of license but also for the restoration of souls." I started thinking on that and see how people were coming in when their driving privilege was suspended and how their lives would be at a pause, because they couldn't get good jobs or they have lost their jobs, because they didn't have their driver license. I thought about how they were coming in broken and upset, and because of that, when the Holy Spirit spoke that in my spirit, I started beginning to see that it was an opportunity to give them hope beyond the restoration of their driving privileges. I began to encourage them. So yes, it became not only a place of restoration for license but also for souls, as they were being healed. Cuts and wounds were being healed, lives were changing right from that place on the corner of 11th and Spring Garden Street. Eventually we had to move out only because the owner wanted to do something different with the property, or at least so he thought. But it was God beginning to move in such a way that I didn't understand.

Most of the time in life, when God begins to move, we don't understand everything at the beginning, but once we take a moment, stop, and listen to His voice, He begins to lead you, guide you, and direct you. Sometimes He doesn't tell or show you all at once. He wants you to have faith. And He wants you to trust and believe him that where He guides, He will provide. And when the owner came to me and my sister and told us that he needed the space, he said that he walked by for two weeks, and it was something that he had never done before. We were grateful and thankful that we were able to make sure that the rent was paid every month on time. We kept the place up. He walked by the office for two weeks while holding this letter that he needed to give to us, but he didn't understand why he was walking by every day and not coming in. But I understood. I understood that God was allowing things to be put in place, so when he came in, sat down, and gave me the letter, I knew instantly that it was a letter that I did not want to see or read. He began to say, "Maryann, you and your sisters have been good tenants here, and I've been looking into some things. I need to occupy the space. He gave us sixty days to vacate. My sister became overwhelmed; she got nauseous. She went down the street to get a ginger ale, came back, and said, "There's a space down the street that has a "for rent sign" on it. We should call them and see about it. It took a few days for me to digest the fact that where we had been for seven years, we will have to pack up and leave from there, not knowing where we were going.

It was truly an emotional time after seeing so many people's lives change in that office through license restoration, through the spirit of God, and through prayer. There was a back room that we used to keep the files, and when the spirit of God came in or when people would be there, talking about their situation, their life experiences, or things that they might have been going through. I observed that at that time, the spirit of God would often lead me to take them in that back room to have prayer with them. I'm reminded of this one time when one of the young men who frequented the area would live outside or live in cars, and he would ask if we needed anything from the store. Do we need him to clean up? To let him know if we need anything. For many days I sought to get him assistance knowing he once served this country. Sometimes you must accept the fact that people must get tired of being tired or worn out.

I always poured into him spiritually and sometimes financially, sometimes not even having to have him do anything. I would just get him something to eat. This one day, he came in and I said, "Come on, let me take you to the back. We are going to go have prayer. It's time for your life to change. You deserve more than this. You deserve better." And I remember taking him in the back room and I began praying. I don't remember all what I said to God, but I do remember this one thing that would never leave my heart nor my mind. I looked to the Lord and said, "Lord, this is your son. You know him. You know all about him and whatever needs to be done. Lord, to cause a change in his life and to get him off the streets, allow it to be done, so that he doesn't have to die in this state. Or whatever your will is for his life, let it be done in the name of Jesus."

Then I looked at him and said, "Do you believe?" and he said, "Yeah, Mary, I believe." He never called me Maryann. He called me Mary. I said, "Amen in Jesus' name, and it is so!!! When you walk out of this office, believe that God has heard us,"

A few days went by, and we noticed that we hadn't seen him for a while. And I began to wonder, *what happened?* It was cold. I thought, well maybe he might have gone into a shelter, because it was so cold, and he was sleeping in cars. Weeks and months went by, but we hadn't seen any signs of him. The neighbors around began to ask, "Have you seen him or hear anything about him?" I said, "No." And all I would think of is when we went into that back room and had prayer. It was six months later that this young man came walking through the door. And I tell you the transformation, the restoration that took place in his life was simply amazing, and now he has his own home. Yes, he's a homeowner, and he has his own vehicle. He works in one of the top hospitals right here in Philadelphia, Pennsylvania!!!!

So, when I talk about restoration, I'm thankful and grateful that being a yielded vessel on Spring Garden Street for over twenty-eight years, I saw restoration in people's lives. I saw restoration in people's marriages, their homes, and their children. During this time, we needed a building for fellowship. We went from my mother-in-law's living room to a Church, where we had begun to fellowship with it. From that time, we left there and went down in my sister Claresa's basement. While in her basement, we were making this transition, and I remember when the Lord began to move and how He began to show things. He began to show how things were going to be happening. The building we moved in was just what we needed. There was another backroom that was simply amazing, because in that back room we didn't need all that space for the operation of our business. I remember my sister Claresa saying, "This could be for the Church!" Instantly the Lord showed her where United Fellowship Deliverance Church would gather.

Our Church would be in the back room; we didn't look like a storefront; we were being tucked away being nurtured and getting prepared to cause a shaking in our city. We looked at the office space as being a place of restoration of driver license and the back being a place reserved for total healing and deliverance.

We opened the Church and started having services in the back room. I began to call it the *Upper Room*. The Lord began to perform miracles. Families were coming in broken; marriages were coming in getting ready to head to divorce court!!! And when they came in for the services, the anointing of God would fall afresh on them, and the Word of God was being released in prayer. The marriages that were headed to divorce were on their way to restoration. Children came in broken, grown up who were still dealing with abandonment issues. They were coming in that place and being healed. They were being delivered and they were set free. Families came in having all kinds of issues among each other—discord, broken hearts, trust issues, and everything that could bring a family down. Alcoholism, drug addiction—all those things came in that back room, and I know the spirit of God resided there, because every family that came to that door and every person that came to alter and called on the name of Jesus, they came into total agreement with the anointing. Lives were being changed. Bodies were being healed. Cancer was being healed. Deliverance was happening. Diseases were healed. Minds were being regulated. Souls were being saved right back there in the *Upper Room*.

When I hear the word *RESTORATION*, I think about how God will allow you to be put in places, not just for what one reason that you might think but also for the glory of God. I also recall when we moved into our new location how the Holy Spirit continued to allow us to see miracles right there in our office. It was around 2008 when another young man came into the office, I was working on getting his driving privileges restored. He was so broken. One day, he just came in and started crying and talking about his issues, his family issues, and what was happening around him. He talked about everything that was going on around him, his children and how he desired to be in their lives and how he was going through a situation with child support. He was at his wit's end. He was ready to give up and was ready to throw in the towel he had the gun in his pocket. He said, "I'm just going to end everything." I said, "No, you cannot.

God has sent you here for a reason, not just for restoration of your license." But he knew this day was going to come when you were going to get tired.

I said, I believe the Lord has sent you here today to pray for restoration of your mind body spirit and soul and not the restoration of your license." I prayed with him, and I told him how important it was for him to start believing God for the changes in his life and for total restoration. All I remember was that he was crying, the tears were falling down his face. I grabbed a piece of paper. I drew a circle with lines coming out from the circle. I said, "This is the Sun, I want you to remember the Son is behind the Sun, and I want you to write on each one of these lines everything that is in your heart or on your mind. When you get finished with that, I want you to fold it up. Then I want you to lift it up to God and say out of your mouth, 'I believe God!!!' Believe Him that everything you have put on the lines, He's going to intervene and change. He's going to cause a miracle to take place in your life." He took the paper, folded it up, put it in his pocket, and said, "Thank you."

We never had the opportunity to discuss his case, because God came in and I felt the anointing rest upon us. A few days went by when he came by the office. This time, he came with a smile and said, "I just wanted to come back to say, 'thank you.' I don't even want to talk about my case. Whatever you got to do, I'll wait for you to call me. But I just came by to tell you, 'Thank you Mom!!!'" That was the beginning of a beautiful relationship.

I knew what the Lord meant when He said that the business will not only be for license restoration but also for restoration of souls. It was sealed in the Heavens. We have seen many souls come through the door to get their driver's license, but they would leave out with something else. They would leave out knowing that Jesus is Lord. They would leave out knowing that Jesus Is a Healer. He's a way maker. He's a miracle worker. He is the Son behind the Sun!!! He will bring change in your life if you just look to him, look beyond the Sun, and see the Son!!!

God is the God of restoration. He would take something that is broken and will cause a miracle to take place. He will bring deliverance, sanctification, and purification.

You may be in a space in your life right now where you don't know what's going on. It maybe dark, and your heart maybe broken. It may seem like there's no coming back. Then it may seem like there's no cure. It maybe sickness, disease, drug addiction, and imprisonment in the mind and of the body in prison, but just know the same God who allowed his anointing to rest upon Spring Garden Street for over twenty-eight years. When people were coming to that back room, *upper room*, they came in one way and when they left, they were different. That same anointing is resting on you right now. Whatever it is, you can just lift your hands to the Lord right now, even while you're reading. Just raise your hands to the Lord right now and believe that He will come right now and rescue you. He will restore you. He will redeem you, because He's, our redeemer. That's how we know that our Redeemer Lives when we see the change in our lives, when we see us coming out of bondage, when we see the change being destroyed, when we see the yolks being destroyed. Sometimes the restoration is not easy. It's likened to the restoration process of regaining your driving privileges. Sometimes it doesn't feel good, and you must be reminded that you must digest the process. Our Lord and Savior Jesus Christ had to digest the process for us to be reconciled with our Father in Heaven. Jesus went to the cross for us to be restored. When you hear the word "restoration" think of yourself receiving back more than what you lost. Know that the Lord has done something greater. The blessing is far more than you ever expected. Be reminded that the Lord said He would bless you. In life, you will go through difficulties. Always remember that this too shall pass!! This is one of the sayings I always share with my clients especially. I'm always telling them it's a restoration day!!!

No matter what's going on, dig deep within and allow your mind to think on being refreshed and rejuvenated, knowing that when you come through, you will be renewed. Yes, even after feeling like you've lost everything!!!! Expect a restoration day!!! Apply it to your mind, body, spirit, and soul. Apply it to your life. If you have lost anything, expect total restoration!!!!

Scripture tells us the Lord spoke, "I will restore you to help and heal your wounds." (Jeremiah 30:17) When the Lord restores, it's always big!!! He does it better than the first time. His mindset and His intentions about us are for us to have a prosperous life. In the book of Job, we see how Job lost everything, even his loved ones. He lost his wife spiritually, because she told him to curse God and die. There will be times when people who are close to you will not and cannot believe like you believe!

Although these all things happened, Job did not turn from his God. In the book of Joel, we see the Lord made a promise that he will restore the years that the palmerworm, cankerworm, and locust had eaten up. Restoration days happened throughout the Bible. No matter what, we must not forget these things and be sure to remember that He's the same God who He was yesterday, is today, and will be forever more. You might be in a place today where you may have lost whether it was physically mentally, financially, or spiritually. I want you to receive it by faith that God said and promised that He would restore you. Every day you speak out your mouth. It's a *RESTORATION Day*!! We should apply it to our lives immediately by faith standing on the promises of God.

# CHAPTER 11

## My Life Is Faith

We must come to an understanding of knowing where we came from and who we came from. When we begin to fully understand this, we will instantly understand why our life is Faith.

We came from a Spirit Being who spoke out of the spirit realm and created things. As the spirit began to speak and create, it began to see you and me in it. The spirit of who we know as God the Father in the midst of darkness had created light. During the creation he said, "Let us make man in our image," and man was created in the likeness of the image being the second part of the spirit. The Spirit breathed breath in the nostril of the image that was created and called it man. Which then became a living soul. He was then placed in a garden where he would have authority and dominion.

Because we come from the Spirit Being, everything that was needed in our lives came with us, and we had to get to a place of an awakening and understand that because everything that we needed here in this earth was created for us to have dominion over and has already been prepared. You came from a spirit that knew everything you would need in the place in which you were placed. Everything you need comes from the spirit. When we understand this, our lives take a miraculous turn. We go from living from a place of anxiety to a place of peace.

There will be times in our life when conflicts, confusion, trials, and tribulations appear because we were placed in a place where there was also a spirit that came to try to take us out of place. The spirit is a force. The Word of God tells us that we wrestle not against flesh and blood but wickedness and principalities in high places. Our lives come with opposition, but the greatest thing to know is that everything we need to defeat it is already placed on the inside of us, and that's faith. Our faith is so powerful that it can destroy the very thing that's trying to destroy us. You must first believe it in your heart and mind. By believing, it shall come to pass with your total trust in the Lord.

Faith is the substance of things hoped for and the evidence of things not seen. The substance is the very thing that we are expecting, however we just can't see it. There are times when we get shaky in our lives, when we can't see the manifestation of a thing. I came to know that we have to believe first in our faith to rely on it. It would take us back to where we come from, and if we can believe that the Spirit spoke out of Himself and created the heavens and the Earth and placed us in it with everything we needed, our faith will be increased.

I began to not only understand this but also accept it. Although I had to walk with my eyes shut although they were open! I couldn't look at what it looked like no matter how hard or bad it seemed. I had to constantly remind myself my God was bigger than anything I was faced with; my life began to change when I received this revelation. At this point, there was nothing in this world that could stop me from believing that whenever I was in need or whatever I needed on this earth that I didn't already have, I just had to walk through the process of life to get it.

Faith is trusting in the invisible God. Faith gives us hope for something to happen; it gives us assurance about things we cannot see. Faith is what God wants, for without it, it's impossible to please Him. Our ancestors pleased God by faith (Hebrews, Chapter 11). Faith is more important to God than deeds and acts…. Noah Abraham Moses, the Woman who had the issue of blood— all had faith, as well as so many others had!

As I journey through my life, I began to take notice of a lot of things as a teenager coming into young adulthood and becoming an adult. I always put some things to the back of my mind meaning I had to block it out. A lot of those things were things that I had to press through in life. I had to digest and process. There was a time when I decided that I needed to sit down and do some deep thinking, realizing my life was not my own. I always remember my siblings and I going to church with either one of my grandfathers. When I think about my life, I think about how my steps were being ordered by the Lord. There were times when I didn't even acknowledge Him. I was singing in the choir at my grandfather David's Church and singing on the choir at Dobbins High School. These were the two places that kept me grounded in my faith since I was introduced to God the Father, Jesus Christ the Son. Later, in my teenage years, I encountered the Holy Spirit. I loved to sing, whether it was R & B or gospel.

I remember we went on tour with Dobbins Mass Choir. We had just got our new robes for the album recording. We were singing "Lord I'm Available to You!!!" While singing, the Holy Spirit fell on me. Nowadays, if you break out in a dance, it's known as catching the Holy Ghost. My encounter with the Spirit falling on me was when I went down and began to worship Him and recalling, not knowing where I was. I was in a place words can't describe. I knew something happened. In the book of Joel, He said, "I will pour out my Spirit upon all flesh." I didn't know where I was. I knew the place I was in wasn't a natural or physical place.

I recall coming out of it and having a nosebleed. They moved me from the choir stand. Some of the sisters from the choir came in to assist me. I never knew what that nosebleed meant; however, I would often think about it. Later as I began to mature in Christ, I learned about deliverance. I knew the Lord allowed deliverance to take place in my life that night. The nosebleed represented the breaking and destroying of yokes in my life, and the blood represented the washing and cleansing of Jesus Christ. I was being delivered from the violation that took place in my life. No matter the level of the violation, when it happens in your life, the enemy defiantly desires to use it to destroy you. When the Lord steps in and causes deliverance to take place, the plan of destruction in which the enemy was devising against you is destroyed!! I continued to sing in the choir and continued to travel with the choir around in Philadelphia, singing in different places. Singing in the choir kept me grounded. I graduated and broke away from the choir, also away from building my relationship with my Lord & Savior Jesus Christ.

As a teenager sometimes you go astray, and I did. I went astray, and I thought I was a grown up and that I could do what I wanted to do. No matter what, I always remember singing "Lord I'm Available to You, My Eyes, My Hands, My Feet, Use Me Lord, I'm Available to You." Going out, I didn't think some of the things that I would experience or would happen, but I knew that they were part of my journey. Some of the things that I went through had to be a part of my journey. As a little girl, I always thought about meeting an anointed singer and pastor from North Carolina. I was singing a lot of her songs along with another anointed female gospel artist. I was singing their songs even while in the world of sin for four years. I would always catch myself singing their songs on Sunday morning. My worldly life didn't last long I soon would find myself back desiring the Church!!!

That's how I know that the Lord was guiding, leading, and directing me. He allowed me to see some things in those four years that, for some people, would have taken almost a lifetime to get free from. I saw a lot of things that plagued our community that I didn't think that I would see. God allowed me to see these things and go through some of them, because he knew that it would be used for his glory. There was a lot of emotional distress that caused me to get into a mess. You know how we often hear people say, "You don't look like what you've been through." WELL!!! I know for sure I certainly didn't. I knew eventually I would have to get it addressed. Four years of being out in the world I discovered that it wasn't a place for me.

When I think about my life is faith, I think about some of the patriarchs of the Bible. I think how the scripture tells us that we only need the faith of a mustard seed—a very small seed!! that's all we need.

I came to a place of knowing that I had to trust God and everything that He said through His Word. I had to receive it spiritually through faith, emotionally I had to open my heart, and mentally I had to have a changed mindset. I had to get the understanding of why I had to go through some hard trials, tribulation and persecution. I had to except the fact that yes, I experienced difficult times and went through a lot of hurt and pain. It wasn't until I accepted these things that I was able to move forward in my life. Unless eventually the devil would try to use these things to destroy the person God created me to be. *MY LIFE IS FAITH*. It's likened unto Noah when God told Noah to build the ark. When he started building, he began to warn the people that it was going to rain. Little did they know that not only was it going to rain but also that it was going to be an unusual rain.

By faith he did what the father told him to do. Everybody was laughing at him, but he knew that he had to build the ark, because he had that much faith in God to know that if God said it, then that's what was going to happen. I think about how and when the Lord would speak to me and tell me to do something, and people would think that I was strange. But my faith allowed me to move forward in whatever He told me to do. If God said it, that's what it was going to be. I had enough faith to speak the things he had told me to say. I learned that we could speak things into existence. My faith tells me that my voice has come with power, and it is powerful enough to create and call things into existence.

I remember speaking things the Holy Spirit would allow me to see. And people would look and try to figure me out. Some even questioned:" Do you really believe that's going to happen?" I used to respond, "Yes, I believe it is going to happen, because God has said it." If He said that I was going to be healed, I believed Him that I would be healed. He said that one of the stripes on Jesus' back was for my healing and that Jesus went to the cross for my healing, I believe that I'm healed. I believe the Lord; I decree and declare healing in my body

The woman who had the issue of blood who bled for so long that she suffered from malnutrition and wasted all her money on all the physicians, still unable to get well. She got very drained and tired. One day, she heard when Jesus was coming by and went to where Jesus was. She crawled to Jesus, and when she got to Jesus, she stopped and touched the Hem of His Garments, she knew that if she just touched it, she would be made whole. Her faith made her whole. Jesus turned around and asked the question, "Who touched me? I felt the virtue go out of me." The disciples being around him said, "There is a crowd of people. What do you mean somebody touched you?" Jesus knew that somebody had touched him with faith. He looked at the woman and told her that her faith has made her whole! My faith leads me to believe!!! I believe every word that has come out from the mouth of God. I will never deny doctors, because I know God gives them knowledge and understanding, however, I know the creator of my body knows His creation, and because He knows that which He created, He will always have the final say over my mind body and soul.

I encourage you to believe every promise that the Lord has made. Open your Word, get into it, and begin to speak the Word of God out of your mouth over your life. Remember, the Word of God tells us that life and death is in the power of our tongue. We must speak life and rebuke death. Remember, Jesus said that He came to give us life, and to give us life more abundantly.

We must have faith, trust, and belief in the God whom we don't see. Jesus has called us blessed. He said that we're blessed because we believe even when we have not yet seen Him. I believe he healed the blind and the lame. I believe that He's a forgiving God. I believe that if you open your mouth and confess your sins, you will be saved.

I think about the time when I first began to evangelize, and the Holy Spirit said that He had placed healing in my hands. I didn't understand why my hands would always get hot and turn red as a tomato. I would feel the anointing in my hands, and it would travel up my arm. The Lord allowed me to know that it was His healing anointing, and that if I laid hands on the sick, they would recover. I had to believe, because there were many people who were around and who didn't believe. I had to believe, and I had to believe for those who didn't believe or didn't have the faith to believe.

I remember when my uncle lay in the hospital, and they told my mother and her siblings they had to remove him from the machine. There was nothing else that they could do. Me along with our Church had just come off our corporate three-day fast. I wouldn't go up to the hospital during the time of the fast. My uncle had been in the hospital in an induced coma for thirty days. I told my mother when she called me. I said, "Don't allow them to do anything. We are going to go pray." I remember that when we came out of prayer and broke fast, I went up to the hospital. I remember going into the hospital room and standing at the foot of my uncle's bed, telling everyone standing in the room how important it was for us to believe and not have any doubt. I asked anybody who did not believe to leave the room. I wasn't being mean; it was just that we needed those who were going to trust and believe in the power of prayer.

Being reminded when Jesus put the crowd out of the ruler's house, where his daughter was dead. Jesus told them to leave the room for she wasn't dead but slept. They laughed at him. Once they were out of the house, He went in the room and took her by the hand, and she rose!! I believed this very thing for my uncle. I began speaking life I remember the Holy Spirit telling me not to pause but just keep praying. I didn't understand what was happening, but I was praying, and I couldn't get distracted. He kept saying Speak Life over him and I began to call my uncle's name and when I called his name, I felt a coolness come over my body. I ended the prayer in Jesus' name and told my family that I had to go. We must believe when we talk with our Lord and Savior and believe with all our heart and soul that He hears, sees, and cares, and that He has already answered our prayer even before we opened our mouth.

I remember leaving the hospital and my mother calling me the next morning—screaming and hollering on the phone. I said, "Mom, what?" She said, "Maryann, he opened his eyes!!" The nurse had called my aunt and told her that he had woken up. My life is Faith. I believe in the power of prayer. I believe that we shall receive anything that we ask in the name of Jesus. Faith means to have that confidence to know in the assurance, to know that God Is, and God can do exceedingly and abundantly, above all that we can ever ask or think!!!

# CHAPTER 12

## It's Not Over

*It's Not Over*! That's what I want you to say to yourself right now. It's not over!!! Say it again, "It's not over!!!!" Say it one more time, "It's not over!!!" Claim it now by faith. We love and serve an invisible God, because He's invisible, and so is his timing!! We don't know when, it's our faith that's within that assures us that He will. We say it believing and trusting Him. You know that it's not over until God says," It's over." We sometimes confess it however we're not really understanding.

When you're in a very hard place and it seems like it's over you, draw from the strength within to open your mouth and shout, "It's not over!!" This is when your faith is in alignment with what you're speaking. The Bible tells us the race is not given to the swift nor the strong but to those who endure to the end.

You're right in the middle of the race and you catch a charley horse, you know how painful they are!!! A charley horse comes on quickly. Most of the time it happens in the leg. Reminds me of the time when I used to have Braxton hicks' contractions while carrying my children. They would hit me without warning!! Every woman who has carried a baby is fully aware of contractions. It's a pain like no other when you start cramping! We often experience charley horses when we've been doing exercise for a long period of time. Especially during the summer months. When we've been out in the heat, not giving our body the proper amount of fluid, and become dehydrated. You have been running your race for a long time, you've been pushing and pulling. Pulling, pulling, and during your pulling you also poured out. During your race, you begin to feel drained. Sometimes you look and ask yourself, "Why am I running this race? Why for so long?" But you understand that it's something deep down on the inside of you. You take your mind off the pressure, contractions, and pains in your muscles, and you keep pushing. You get these charley horses, you look up, and you see yourself almost at the finishing line!!! Are you going to quit because of the pain? Or are you going to press past the pain? I know sometimes the pain can be very intense; at such times, call on Jesus!! See yourself finishing the race and being victorious.

You may be in that very place right now, or you may just be coming out of it or heading in that direction. Either way, just shout victory right now!! The Lord will pour out his anointing and give you supernatural strength to endure and finish. By faith, you must believe that you have already won! You must have the winner's mentality.

This reminds me of when I was running in one of my spiritual races, and, in the middle, I caught a charley horse, it felt like everything was in that pain— hurt, disappointment, betrayal, fear, pressure, depression, darkness, anxiety. I wanted to give up. Yes, I did. The pain and the pressure were so intense that some nights I wanted to get in my car and just keep driving. In 2007, my business took a major turn due to the court system. We had just gone into a recession. There was no money in the bank and having to break $5 down in half …. one time a $1.50 in half. The recession was meant to take me into depression. Many referrals were coming in, however, we had to hold the cases, because there was nothing we could do. You know honesty is the best policy.

We could have taken cases and had them on hold until something changed in the system, however, we made the decision to tell our clients that nothing could be done at this time. This was very hard to do, because it felt as though we were letting our clients down. That was a major charley horse. Yes, we suffered a huge financial loss, however, I remember saying that something good must come out of this. I reminded myself that all things work together for the good to them who love and are called by the Lord. Yes, although it didn't look like it was going to work out good, I kept believing it would, and it did!!! To me, it was the greatest time spiritually. Although during this mile in the race we couldn't provide our clients with the restoration of their driver license, we truly were able to provide hope and pray for the restoration of their souls!!! To see grown men come in crying, because they may have lost their jobs because of not having their driver license or being laid off due to the recession, some losing their homes and families, was extremely difficult, however, the Holy Spirit occupied our office!! The anointing always showed up through prayer and comforting during a time of releasing an encouraging word! Although we were going through challenging times ourselves, we knew sometimes some clients came to the office just for peace and comfort. We had to keep our eyes on the finishing line that was nowhere to be seen. That allowed me to know that it wasn't over. The business was still in the race.

One night, I couldn't go to sleep. I tossed and turned, and then I got out of my bed. I went downstairs to my living room and began to seek the Lord for wisdom, knowledge, and understanding. I humbled myself in the presence of the Lord. The Holy Spirit gave me peace and the pressure that was on me instantly left. He began to give me strategies on how we could begin taking cases and remain successful and true to our clients. I didn't procrastinate, I began writing them down and moved out with faith. The next day, I presented the strategy to the attorney. He looked at me and said, "Maryann, what am I going to do with you??" I replied, "Do as the Lord has instructed me to do…." Hallelujah, the Lord breathed on it and the business began to flourish in the middle of the recession. I remember being encouraged in my spirit, hearing, "The recession was meant for depression; however, I'm going to use it for your possession."

I had been asking the Lord for a new car; however, I didn't desire to have a car note. He directed me to go!!! I spoke with my husband and shared with him my desire. We went into agreement and prayed. He said the Holy Spirit showed him how I can pay my brand-new car off!!! I drove off the lot with twenty-one miles on it. I purchased the car in February 2007, and in May

2007, my brand new 2007 Nissan Sentra was paid in full!!! If I had given in to the charley horse, I would have quit and missed my blessing!!! If I would have kept my eyes on the recession and what was happening in the judicial system, I would have given up the business. IT'S NOT OVER!! Therefore, you must keep speaking to yourself and confess that He who has begun a good work in me will complete it!!! I will finish.

Sometimes the Lord will allow some things to happen during the race. This is for you to pick up the additional blessings. Don't get distracted by the charley horse. You may not see your way coming out victorious, but you must open your mouth and shout (Hebrews 11 and 1). NOW faith is the substance of things hoped for the evidence of things not seen. You may think it's the end, but you must know that it's not over until God says it is over and know that finish doesn't always mean over….

Remember, Jesus' mission down here on earth was finished, but it wasn't over for Him!! He had to come back to reveal Himself, so the scripture would be fulfilled. He's now sitting on the right-hand side of Abba Father, making intercession for us!! Whatever you do, trust and believe that you have the *victory in darkness.* Believe in your heart and have the mindset of finishing strong. Say, "It's not over." You must align your mind; you must know that when the scripture tells us let this mind be in you that is also in Christ Jesus. Know the Jesus' mindset was always victory. I never accepted defeat, although sometimes it appeared like I was going to be defeated. I never accepted it.

I always think about when my Lord Jesus always looked to His Father when He needed strength. He looked at His Father when He was ready to lay hands to heal. He looked at His Father when He was walking through the valley of the shadow of death. He always looked to His Father. We must look to our father. Knowing the Word of God tells us we are the head and not the tail and that we will be the lender and not the borrower. You must get it down in your soul that it's not over until God says it's over. Jesus went all the way to the cross with everything he had to go through being betrayed with a kiss from Judas, he had to go through being denied by one who he walked with, whipped beat all night long. Jesus carried his own cross; He went into places where He knew it was dark and dangerous. He kept going because He knew that it wasn't over until God said it was over!!! On his way up to be crucified, his mindset was victory.

He spoke victory even when He told them when they were in the temple. He said, if you destroy this temple in three days, I will raise it back up. And they thought He was talking about the natural temple. He was talking about Himself!!! Speaking in the spiritual realm of FAITH—being raised up, and that's what you have to believe. You must have the mindset of victory and that no matter what comes against you, you're going to rise!!! Jesus died on the cross, while on the cross, He looked to the heavens and said, "Father, forgive them, for they know not what they do." You're going to go through your race of life and people are going to do all manner of evil against you, but you must pray and ask the Lord to forgive them for they know not what they do. They don't know what they're doing, because if they really knew what they were doing, they wouldn't do it…. Sometimes, it's beneficial for them to do what they have done. The betrayal and hurt in my life pushed me in the presence of my Lord and Savior Jesus Christ.

Jesus stayed there on the cross; He knew that He had victory, even during death. He had victory in His darkest hour. He knew that it was victory after all His work was done. He had run the race. He looked up to the heavens and said that it was finished. He knew it was done, but He couldn't say that it was finished until God said that it was over. When He said it was finished, it was just finished down here on Earth. He knew in three days that He would be resurrected. This is key you MUST know!

You're going to go through some things in life, and you will have to push through. Continue running the race, because when you get to the finishing line, you are going to be able to stand and tell somebody about the race!! You will be able to stand and tell them what you went through. Jesus departed and went back to glory; however, He didn't leave the disciples empty. He filled them with His Spirit! It's not over until God gives you everything that He prepared for you down here on this earth. It's not over until you get it; keep pushing. You must keep praying, keep believing, keep fasting, keep pressing, and keep running, even when the charley horses come, even when the contractions come, even when the pain comes, even when it feels like you're going to pass out, and even when you're in the fire. When the heat is turned up and its darker than dark, it's causing you to be dehydrated and exhausted!! You must keep running the race, keep expecting victory!!!! Can't you see the finishing line? If you do not see the Finishing Line, it means that you have more running to do. You cannot give up as soon as you begin to see the finishing line. That is where you take a deep breath. You say, I'm almost there. I must keep going. I must persevere. I see the finishing line." Soon you can say, "This race is over." Gather your strength and get ready for the next one.

I do not know how many races you are going to have in life, but just know that there are going to be many races, and in every race, the Lord knows the condition of each one. Remember, He said all things work together for our good!!! And if you fall in the races, just like the Word of God tells us, a just man falls seven times, however, He gets back up. In the middle of the race, when the charley horse hits you, just grab your leg when that pain hits you on your side. Just grab your side when the thorn is in your flesh; keep going. Sometimes the thorn remains in your flesh to keep you humble. Paul asked for it to be removed three times, the Lord said, "My grace is sufficient for you. It's not over; keep going; you got to keep believing; you got to keep trusting!! Shout aloud now, "MY LIFE IS FAITH!!"

Don't get distracted by who is on the sideline, sometimes people will be on the sidelines, looking at your situation, trying to figure out how you're still running and trying to figure out how are you running with this charley horse when you should have lost your breath and fainted on the track. They become a distraction. Don't look to your left or to your right; keep looking forward. Don't allow the distractions to confuse you as to who's cheering you on. When you're running your race, you have your cheerleaders on the sidelines as well as your opponent's cheerleaders. Sometimes they stand on your side as if they are cheering you on the whole time when they're praying that the charley horse causes you to collapse. They show up as the enemy, watching to see if you're going to win with a wonder and question: Why he didn't give up or why she didn't give up? Why didn't he slow down? Why didn't she slow down? Oh! I just knew that trip from their shoelaces was going to do it, or that scratch on their knee was going to stop them.

Think about all the life experiences that you had the opportunity to learn from. Remain focused and keep your eyes on the Lord. Keep your ears open to him. Be reminded of the scripture when it tells us that you're more than a conqueror and that you can do all things through Christ Jesus, who strengthens you. Remember, you already have the victory while you're running! His name is Jesus!!! When it looks dark in your life and when things aren't going your way, you must stand firm in faith like Jesus! When you speak out of your mouth, it is finished. What you're really saying is, "God, I know you're going to turn this situation around." You must decree and declare, "Lord you're going to heal my body, and I know you're going to restore my family." Always remember to speak victory in darkness. The Lord is faithful, and He will complete what He has begun in you.

What I love about my life is faith is that all I must do is continue to BELIEVE which I wholeheartedly do in any situation, expecting nothing but total victory, even in darkness. Jesus spoke the Words "I'm with you always, even unto the end of the world."

Therefore, I decree and declare, *"MY LIFE IS FAITH"*, because even when it's dark and it looks like it's over, it's not over!!" *I HAVE VICTORY IN DARK-NESS!*!!

# DEDICATION

The Trinity

To Abba Father, My Lord & Savior Jesus Christ
and the Holy Spirit it's because of you

My Life Is Faith

My Strawberry Patch

(Granddaughters)

Ealajiah (Snappy) Ealissa (Happy) & Ea 'Siyah (Jolly)

And Future Grandchildren

Trust in the Lord with all your hearts always acknowledge Him and He shall direct your paths.

Continue in the Gospel of Jesus Christ

# ACKNOWLEDGEMENTS

To my amazing husband & friend Gregory Sr.

Thank you for your LOVE, UNDERSTANDING, ENCOURAGEMENT, being my number one supporter truly being a part of My Life Is Faith, I LOVE YOU FOREVER.

To my daughter & son

My Queen Claresa (Boop) thank you for always motivating, inspiring and always praying for me!!! My King Gregory Jr. (Daad) thank you for bringing out the warrior in me!!! The love I have for the two of you words will never ever be able to describe.

To my father & mother

Thank you for giving me life!!!! Without the two of you there would be no me!!

Thanks for keeping me on the steps protecting, loving, caring and always believing in me!!

*In Loving Memory*

Of

*My Grandfathers William Hellams & David Williams*

Thank you for introducing me to Jesus Christ and keeping me in Church!!

My Angel Aunt

Thank you for desiring to spend time with me. Only God
knows how I wished you and those children made it out
of the fire. I will forever carry you in my heart!!

*Mother-In-Law Pastor Louise Nathaniel*

I'm still pressing on!! Thank you for seeing in me that which I didn't see!!

*Uncle Johnell & Spiritual Daughter Eva Marie*

Thank you for your unlimited support & love for me and in the ministry

Sis. Eva!!! Women Worshipping at the Water made it in a book!!

*My Big Poppa (Bonus Dad),*

Thank you for always cheering me on!!! I'm glad to know that you had
an opportunity to hear parts of My Life Is Faith!! I remember sitting
on the living room couch and you saying, "Alright Now"! Every time
I stand to minister, I will hear you say Preach that Word daughter!!

All of you will forever be in my heart!!!